Atomic Marbles

& BRANDING IRONS

A Guide to Museums, Collections, and Roadside Curiosities in Washington and Oregon

Harriet Baskas
and Adam Woog

SASQUATCH BOOKS
SEATTLE

Printed in the United States of America.

Cover design and illustrations: Scott Hudson
Interior design: Scott Hudson
Composition: Seattle Weekly Typesetting

Library of Congress Cataloging in Publication Data

Baskas, Harriet.
    Atomic marbles and branding irons : a guide to museums,
collections, and roadside curiosities in Washington and Oregon /
Harriet Baskas and Adam Woog.
        p. cm.
    Includes index.
    ISBN 0-912365-79-X : $12.95
    1. Washington (State)—Guidebooks. 2. Oregon—Guidebooks.
3. Museums—Washington (State)—Guidebooks. 4. Museums—Oregon—
Guidebooks. 5. Collectors and collecting—Washington (State)—
Guidebooks. 6. Collectors and collecting—Oregon—Guidebooks.
I. Woog, Adam, 1953– . II. Title.
F889.3.B37—1993
917.9504'43—dc20   93-21871
                                                                         CIP

Sasquatch Books
1931 Second Avenue
Seattle, Washington 98101
(206) 441-6202

Contents

Oregon

Acknowledgments

Thanks:

To the collectors and curators who let us poke around in their stuff;

To our spouses, Karen Kent and Ross Reynolds, for patience and support;

To Stu Witmer and Griggs Irving, for getting the ball rolling;

To road companions Alan Woog, Ralph and Ione Turman, Joe Kogel, and Mary Catherine Lamb;

To tipsters and museum-lovers Archie Satterfield, Hu Blonk, Bob Roseth, Richard Engeman, Sandy Polishuk, Jerry Richard, Tom Cole, Carol Jo Nance and Clyde Horn, Linda Essex, Paul and John Klein, Mary Orr, Nancy Compau, Stephanie Irving, David Mahler and Anne Focke, and Gordon Black.

And special thanks to the Sasquatch staff (Anne Depue, Chad Haight, Emily Hall, and computer whiz Jenny Dixey) and their colleagues photographer Karna Steelquist, copy editor Phyllis Hatfield, and designer Scott Hudson.

—A.W. and H.B.

On Collecting

Give me a museum and I'll fill it.— Pablo Picasso

The Northwest has long been famous for the beauty and majesty of its great outdoors. But some of the greatest wonders here are found *indoors*—and they have been decidedly manufactured or collected by human hands. This book is a guide to some of these "civilized" wonders: from a museum of 80-odd vacuum cleaners in Portland to a pair of prehistoric sandals in Salem; from the world's largest rosary collection in Stevenson to a former hobo's House of Poverty in Moses Lake. Such collections, falling somewhere between conventional museums and Aunt Ann's shelf of thimbles, salvage things that most of us might pass over or throw away. They serve as collective memories for communities and illuminate overlooked histories—social, political, technological, and personal. Best of all, they're fun.

Writing this book changed the way we think about collections and collectors. Our plan was to swing quickly through Washington and Oregon, stopping here and there to glance over a county museum or poke through a barn full of treasures. To our surprise and delight, we soon found ourselves in serious discussions over the very definition of a museum. Does any odd place filled with strange things constitute a collection? What do these strange things tell us about the collectors as well as ourselves? Why collect this stuff, and why on earth put it on display?

For some, a private collection begins as a hobby but eventually devours a shelf, a room, the garage, and, in time, a home and a life. In order to save a marriage, or a reputation, people find themselves moving collections into rented spaces and declaring their "museums" open to visitors. Sometimes a collection takes on such historical or cultural importance—such as Bob Weatherly's branding irons in Asotin—that it is donated to a "real" museum so that it can be shared with the public.

For others, collecting is purely sentimental. Many people told us that the items in their collections remind them of places they visited, work they did, people they knew, or events that changed their lives. Others admitted that their motivation was the challenge of the search or the satisfaction that comes from assembling complete sets. Not surprisingly, some people simply answered our question "Why collect this?" with another question: "Why not?"

The professionals and volunteers who operate community museums know that even the objects that seem the most trivial can illuminate and deepen our understanding of our ancestors and past events. At first, we passed quickly by the ever-present cases of china teacups, porcelain dolls, and arrowheads, hurrying over to look at the meteorites, the two-headed calves, and the taxidermied bears. But in time we came to appreciate the humbler stuff. As we learned about the hardships the earliest settlers endured to get here, we understood that the remarkable thing about those china teacups and dolls is that they, and the people who brought them, survived the trip at all. We came to marvel at the skill with which Native Americans made arrowheads that have lasted 10,000 years and at the accuracy with which they fired them day after day in the wilderness.

We knew we were close to the essence of collecting when we came upon Mamie Thompson's electric stove at the Big Bend Historical Society Museum in Wilbur, Washington. It seemed, at first, a silly item to keep in a museum. But when we envisioned the day that newfangled stove arrived in town, we began to understand how objects can bring us closer to the past and trigger our imaginations. Think of Mamie's excitement as the shiny appliance is delivered; consider her neighbor's envy as she peeks through her kitchen curtain pretending not to care, and the cynical talk over morning coffee at the general store as wagers are placed on how long it will take for the dang thing to break down. Mamie's stove represents a pivotal time, a community moving into the modern age. It's an apt symbol, for us, of the charm and importance of collecting.

We also learned that the people behind the museums are often the real treasures. It's one thing to see an old pair of shoes in a glass case and wonder how the owner could walk with her toes scrunched into a sharp point. It's quite another to have an 80-year-old museum volunteer show you those very same shoes and hear stories of her grandmother walking many uncomfortable miles in them. In the same way, the House of Poverty would be just another jumble of odd and unrelated things if not for its ex-hobo collector, who weaves each piece into a fascinating and possibly true-life story.

To keep the book to a reasonable size, we pared the list of entries down to our favorites; what remains is a carefully selected but highly subjective collection of collections. In some cases, such as museums devoted to military or timber history, we selected one or two representative examples. General historical museums were included if they had especially interesting aspects, but we couldn't list them all.

We concentrated on lesser-known collections and institutions, but some mainstream destinations made the final cut. The Boeing Everett plant earns a place of honor here because of its otherworldliness—the sheer size of the objects on view made us feel like we were on another planet. In well-known institutions, such as the Tacoma Art Museum or the Burke Museum, we focused on a single collection of special interest. On the other hand, we included a number of roadside attractions—among them such delightfully uncategorizable places as the Church of Elvis in Portland, the Walker Rock Garden in Seattle, and Dick and Jane's Spot in Ellensburg. To us, they represent irresistible obsessions—an important element of any good collection.

Probably the biggest lesson we learned during the writing of this book is the joy of serendipity. We heard about many of these spots from friends, colleagues, and helpful locals, but we simply stumbled upon many of them as well. Some of our best experiences were completely unexpected: stopping by a small museum in a quiet backwater, thinking it wouldn't be much—only to find that it was a very special place indeed, thanks to the generosity and knowledge of the people in charge. Sometimes we discovered overlooked gems in the middle of well-trodden paths, and sometimes the luck came in the form of astonishing places, hidden virtually in our neighborhoods, that had been waiting patiently for us to find them.

We hope this serendipity rubs off on you. It's one thing to read about a place and its holdings, something else to visit it. But the real pleasure—and the real learning—comes when you find something new and uncharted in some unlikely spot. We hope this book will prompt you to do some discovering of your own.

—H.B. and A.W.

NOTE: Our information is as accurate as possible, but—especially with small or private museums, which may be operated by a single person—things do change. It's always best, therefore, to call ahead.

Did we overlook one of your favorites? Please write to us care of Sasquatch Books, 1931 Second Avenue, Seattle, Washington 98101.

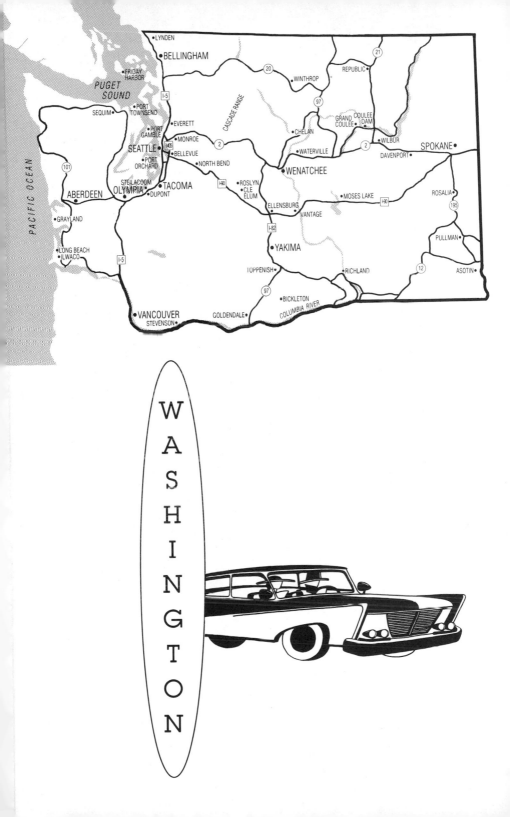

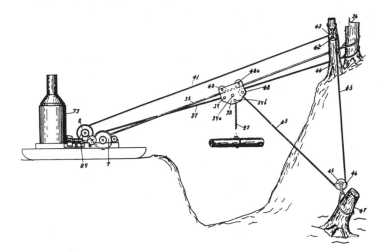

Lumberjacks and Steam Donkeys

ABERDEEN
McMeekin Logging Equipment Collection

Jack McMeekin, a retired logger who specialized in topping trees, claims he has the largest collection of timber-related equipment in the state, and we're not here to doubt him. One of his guided tours will tell you a tremendous amount about the history of that venerable and endangered industry, Northwest logging.

At McMeekin's house you'll see a steam donkey, used to haul logs in the days before aerial logging made it "easy." On hand also are a variety of massive chains, toothy saws, and springboards, which early loggers rammed into the bases of Douglas firs and stood on for better purchase. McMeekin's springboards are mounted in a stump that stands 15 feet high and has a circumference of almost 50 feet. He had it specially imported and says that his wife nearly had a fit when she saw him haul it in.

You can't miss the McMeekin place—just look for the house

and yard littered with gigantic chains and huge pieces of machinery. It's a brightly colored display — McMeekin regularly coats the machinery with rust-resistant paint (at Christmastime he likes to string lights all around).

McMeekin Logging Equipment Collection • 6612 Olympic Highway, Aberdeen, Washington 98520 • (206) 532-3076
Admission: Free. **Hours:** By appointment only, unless you just want to look from the road. **To get there:** The house is roughly midway between Montesano and Aberdeen; as you drive west on Highway 12, it will be on the north side of the street "between the blinker lights."

ICU2: Branding Irons

ASOTIN
Asotin County Historical Society Museum

C attle and other livestock often are identified to establish ownership, control disease, track purebred bloodlines, or determine age. Sometimes they are tattooed, or their ears are notched or tagged, but the most common method of animal identification is a mark burned into the animal's hide with a hot iron.

Egyptian farmers used the technique 4,000 years ago, and it was introduced to North America by the explorer Hernando Cortés in the sixteenth century. As ranching spread throughout the American West, the varieties of animal branding became as colorful, individualized, and complex as medieval heraldry symbols.

The Asotin County Historical Society Museum, in the southeast Washington town of Asotin, has an excellent collection of branding irons that illustrates some of the history behind these tools. About 200 pieces are on long-term loan from Robert P. Weatherly, a retired cattleman who writes a regular history column for the local newspaper. As Weatherly tells it, "I got into this a number of years ago, when a fellow was telling me that he had bought several homesteads and picked up a few branding irons. He said a person from Seattle was going to buy them and sell them in an antique store, that people were putting them in the rec rooms of their houses. Well, that seemed like a hell of an idea—they're a kind of history of this region, and it seemed a shame to let them go."

When Weatherly began asking around, "it seemed like everyone had a few old irons lying around that they didn't know who they belonged to." He added garage sale and antique store finds to these donations. He also collected old brand books, the official gazettes that publish registered brands, which have helped him track down and identify long-unused marks.

The typical iron in the Asotin collection is 3 to 4 feet long. Horse brands are relatively small, usually less than 2 inches high; horses are usually branded under the mane to avoid spoiling their appearance. A calf brand may be 4 inches high, and, since brands expand as animals grow, some full-size animals have foot-high brands on their sides. Date brands are sometimes used on the jaw to indicate the year an animal was born. Weatherly says, "Let's say you look at an animal and it has a 2 on its jaw. That'll tell you right away how old that animal is. And if you can't tell the difference between a cow that was born in '82 or '92, then you shouldn't be in the business."

Many of the irons in the Asotin museum date from the days

of hand-forging; electricity and welding came relatively late to the region's farms, in many cases (including Weatherly's) not until after the Second World War.

Most of the irons come from ranches in Asotin and Garfield counties, but the museum also has a few from outside the region, including one brand from an early Spanish settler on Whidbey Island with an intricate abstract design. "You pick it up and look at it and you don't know what the hell it is; all you can tell is that it's a branding iron from someone with an imagination," says Weatherly. There is also a series of irons that became a community joke among a group of ranchers in Montana: the first one reads IC, the second ICU, and the third ICU2.

Asotin County Historical Society Museum • 3rd and Fillmore, Asotin, Washington 99402 • (509) 243-4659
Admission: Free; donations accepted. Hours: Tues–Sat 10am–4pm. To get there: At 3rd and Fillmore, turn right at the grocery store.

Raggedy Andy Meets Shirley Temple

BELLEVUE
The Rosalie Whyel Museum of Doll Art

D oll collecting has always been popular, but in the past 20 years nostalgia for simpler times and well-made items has made this hobby even more fashionable. A visit to the Rosalie Whyel Museum of Doll Art is an object lesson in seeing dolls as serious art as well as simple playthings. Whyel, who comes from a wealthy coal family in Alaska, built a collection so large and renowned that in 1992 it inspired her to construct a huge, two-story, Victorian-style building, both to house the collection and to enable her to share it with others.

Susan Pickel Hedrick, Whyel's friend and the museum curator, says there are bigger doll collections on display in other
American museums, but none she's seen includes such intricate
labeling or detailed displays as those here. She's especially fond of
the doll "vignettes," showcases that are designed to display as
many dolls as possible and to demonstrate various phases of doll
history. Her favorites are the bevy of more than 20 "Baby Dolls"
that fill one case, and the "Doll Hospital," which includes an X ray
of a doll "patient." We enjoyed the case that uses early homemade
and manufactured dolls to explain how materials such as rubber,
metal, porcelain, and even plastic changed doll-making technology.

An English doll from 1690 is the oldest and perhaps rarest
piece in the museum. A storytelling doll with a swivel head has the
sweet face of Red Riding Hood on one side, the Big Bad Wolf on
another, and Grandma on a third. Another rare doll, the anatom-
ically incorrect "Bebe Gourmand" model, made in 1881, can "eat"
a biscuit inserted into her mouth. The biscuit falls down a tube in
the doll's body and comes out a hole in one of her feet.

Dollhouses and rare dollhouse miniatures fill one full-sized
room upstairs, while downstairs is reserved for mass-market character dolls such as Barbie, Shirley Temple, G.I. Joe, Mickey Mouse,

and Bart Simpson, as well as one-of-a-kind contemporary artist dolls from around the world. Throughout the museum, surprise pull-out drawers and closets stretch the available display area and satisfy (somewhat) the urge to touch something.

Although admission to this museum is a bit steep and most everything is behind glass, children will love it, especially the magical "toy attic" where the doll-sized train set, rocking horse, and rocking chair periodically come to life. While the kids are running from one exhibit case to another, adults will appreciate the well-placed benches that encourage closer inspection of more elaborate dolls, viewing of informative short films, and pondering the museum-quality treasures you might own yourself if you hadn't thrown out the dolls you or your children outgrew.

The Rosalie Whyel Museum of Doll Art • 1116 108th Avenue NE, Bellevue, Washington 98004 • (206) 455-1116
Admission: $5 for adults, discounts for children and senior citizens. **Hours:** Mon–Wed and Fri–Sat 10am–5pm, Thurs 10am–8pm, Sun 1pm–5pm. **To get there:** The museum is located near downtown Bellevue. From I-405 take the NE 8th (westbound) exit and look for signs leading you to the museum.

Edson-Booth Bird Collection

BELLINGHAM
Whatcom Museum

John M. Edson of Bellingham was an amateur ornithologist who collected and mounted birds from the 1890s until his death in 1954. Edward Edson (no relation) was the mayor of nearby Lynden for 14 years and also the owner of that town's City Drug Store. He was inspired by his drugstore chain—Owl Drugs—to collect owls, which were mounted and displayed in his store. Edward J. Booth operated a taxidermy shop in Bellingham for many years, prepared mounts for both John Edson and Edward

Edson, and collected stuffed birds. The samples collected by these three men form the Edson-Booth Collection of the Whatcom Museum: over 800 specimens, primarily of Pacific Northwest birds, representing some 200 species.

It's a gorgeous collection, complete with up-to-date information. Roughly 570 birds are on permanent display, with the others available for viewing by interested patrons. Photo backdrops give a sense of what the birds looked like in the wild; birds are also displayed on long shelves behind glass.

Twenty-eight species of local wild duck are exhibited in groups (surface-feeding ducks, bay ducks, sea ducks, and stiff-tailed ducks). There are birds of prey (including hawks, owls, falcons, and eagles) and six varieties of woodpeckers. Waterbirds are represented by loons, grebes, pelicans, and swans. There are gallinaceous birds (heavy-bodied, chickenlike creatures such as grouse and quail); perching birds (a large group that includes crows, thrushes, warblers, thrushes, tanagers, swallows, jays, magpies, and chickadees); shorebirds (among them plovers, sandpipers, and killdeer); and more. Two birds that have been much in the news recently—the spotted owl and the marbled murrelet—attract special attention. Non-native birds, such as the nearly extinct great white whooping crane, can also be seen here.

Whatcom Museum • 121 Prospect Street, Bellingham, Washington 98225 • (206) 676-6981

Admission: Free. **Hours:** Tues–Sun 12pm–5pm. **To get there:** From I-5 take the Lakeway exit; go west on Lakeway, which becomes Holly. At the three-way intersection, take a right onto Prospect and go two blocks.

Bluebirds of Happiness

BICKLETON
Bickleton Bluebird Trail

Bickleton, in Klickitat County, is the self-proclaimed Bluebird Capital of the World, being home to two types of bluebirds: the all-blue mountain bluebird and the red-breasted Western bluebird. Both are migratory and head south as far as Mexico every October, returning to Klickitat County in mid-February. The spring mating season is the best time to see them.

In the mid-1960s, Jess and Elva Brinkerhoff began erecting bluebird houses, and eventually developed what became known as the Bickleton Bluebird Trail. Their first birdhouse—still standing—was a one-gallon tin can nailed to a tree. The Brinkerhoffs eventually placed more than 1,500 wooden houses across 150 square miles of eastern Klickitat County. Most are white houses with blue roofs, nailed to the tops of fence posts and clearly visible to motorists.

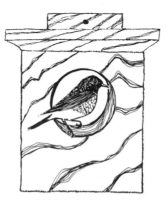

After Elva's death in 1985, the people of Bickleton took over the task of maintaining the trail. Volunteers build new houses, repair existing ones, and clean each house in the fall. They say that birds often wait impatiently for the last nail to be driven into new houses, occupying them just seconds after completion.

Bickleton Bluebird Trail • (509) 896-2344 • **To get there:** A drive along any of the roads around Bickleton will take you past dozens of bluebird houses.

False Teeth and Rattlers

BICKLETON
The Whoop N Holler Museum

The commercial district of Bickleton, in the Horse Heaven Hills of south central Washington, consists of the Bickleton Country Kitchen Restaurant and the Bluebird Tavern. The restaurant has great homemade pie, and the tavern claims to be the oldest one in the state. One of the items for sale in the Country Kitchen is a lapel button that reads, "I went to the edge of the horizon . . . and the sign said: Bickleton, 10 miles."

To get to the Whoop N Holler Museum, go to Bickleton . . . and then go 12 miles more, to the home of Lawrence and Ada Ruth Whitmore.

Lawrence and Ada Ruth grew up in families that homesteaded around Bickleton before the turn of the century, and they have strong ties to the area. Ada Ruth is especially active in the community, has written several books of local history, and was instrumental in the movement that made Bickleton the Bluebird Capital of the World. But her most important link with Bickleton's past is the museum that she and Lawrence created—an eccentric collection that lets the Whitmores link their family stories with local history, and tell the public about it, too.

When Ada Ruth married Lawrence in 1947, his family was already collecting everything: "They'd save the wrapper from a piece of meat. He had a Studebaker, and I had a trunkful of stuff too. After that, it just mushroomed." Since then, they've filled several large outbuildings with inherited stuff and acquired enough vintage cars to cover a hillside. They recently bought an old schoolhouse and the local Grange hall, which they plan to move onto their property to alleviate the space problem at their cramped museum.

Everything comes with a story. Mounted on the wall is the tin bathtub that Lawrence and Ada Ruth used the first three years they were married. There's the 1927 Studebaker they courted in. And here's a sepia-tinted photograph of a heavily mustached man with snakes draped around his arms and neck: "Lawrence's grandfather Churchill and 13 live rattlesnakes," according to the caption. Ada says he often carried snakes around, and they never did bite him.

You can see everything from hand-carved doll furniture to an electrified metal lunch-box—plug it in and it heats your food. The collection also includes Coke cans collected from around the world by the Whitmore kids, a tarantula skin, home remedies sold to successive generations of Whitmores by traveling salesmen, and a hearse equipped with a wicker basket that Ada Ruth says was used for separated body parts. The Whitmores are always adding to their holdings; when we visited, they'd recently turned up the false teeth of a relative who had died in 1917.

The Whoop N Holler Museum • **1 Whitmore Road, Bickleton, Washington 99322** • **(509) 896-2344**

Admission: $3 for adults, discounts for groups and families. **Hours:** Tues–Sun; call ahead for hours. **To get there:** The Whitmore farm is 12 miles south of Bickleton and 11 miles north of Roosevelt on East Road. Watch for the hillside full of cars and a sign in front.

𝒯𝒽𝑒 𝐵𝓁𝒶𝒸𝓀 𝒞𝓇𝑜𝓈𝓈

CHELAN
Chelan County Museum

In 1904, Cashmere took its name from a verse by Sir Thomas Moore that referred to the "Vale of Kashmir, with its roses, the brightest that ever gave." The town still has a storybook feel that extends to the county museum. This huge complex was built entirely by volunteers and features material from central Washington dating back 9,000 years. There is also an entire pioneer village out back stocked with authentic buildings, and a colorful wildflower garden planted at the museum's front door.

The museum's nationally known Willis Carey collection of Indian artifacts and pioneer relics includes photos of the Wenatchi tribe and Northwest Coast Indians, as well as stone tools, baskets, and porcupine-hair and buffalo-horn headdresses. One display case is filled with Hudson's Bay Co. trading items, including thimbles, blankets, twists of tobacco, brass, glass, and copper buttons.

Ask to see the black stone double cross Mrs. Lois Cooke found in her garden in 1941. According to the newspaper clipping posted nearby, Mrs. Cooke, who lived about 6 miles downriver from Wenatchee, "worked for 50 years in the same garden and one day she saw a black tip sticking out of the ground." The double cross, a rare Native American artifact estimated to be 1,500 to 2,000 years old, lies alongside a photo of Mrs. Cooke in her garden.

While the upstairs exhibit hall is impressive for the sheer depth of its collection, it's the special touches on the lower level of the museum that won our hearts. A display of fossilized wood here includes a young piece "just 13 million years old"! And among the lovingly created, natural-looking dioramas filled with taxidermied birds and wild forest animals, a trapper sits in his low-ceilinged cabin, getting ready to go hunting.

Just beyond the trapper's cabin, as if to prove that the pioneer settlers brought culture out West along with their farming tools, there's a display of musical instruments, dolls, toys, and a remarkable case stuffed with family heirlooms. The polished silver, glass pitchers, and inlaid wooden boxes include "something special from every old-time family," says the volunteer on duty.

Chelan County Museum • 600 Cottage Avenue, Cashmere, Washington 98815 • (509) 782-3230
Admission: By donation. **Hours:** Apr–Oct: Mon–Sat 10am–4:30pm, Sun 1pm–4:40pm. **To get there:** Follow Cottage Avenue through downtown Cashmere over the Wenatchee River to the museum. Or look for signs on US 2 at Cashmere for Cottage Avenue and the museum.

Things on Our Windowsills

CHELAN
Lake Chelan Historical Museum

Chelan is a small resort town often overrun by tourists. On the day we visited, the streets and restaurants were full but the museum was empty, giving the two volunteers on duty plenty of time to answer our questions, point out their favorite displays, and reminisce about the good old days.

Most everyone's favorite section here is the large display of local apple-crate labels arranged in a tall, wall-mounted scrapbook. While the museum in Wenatchee has many more labels and the Yakima Valley Museum and others have fine collections, we spied some new favorites here, including Appletizin, Don't Worry, Young Love, Plen Tee Color, and Quality Talks.

Along with the requisite arrowhead and mineral collections, this museum has made room for the movie projector and the stage curtain from the town's old Ruby Theater. The curtain still sports painted advertisements for local businesses. Downstairs, along a narrow corridor, look for dioramas of pioneer life, Knut Hjelvik's 6-pound raccoon coat, Hudson's Bay Co. trading items, and a homemade banjo with a woman's intricately carved head on the back.

Two exhibits reminded us of the importance that cluttered, attic-like museums like this play in a town's collective memory. In 1944, the day before Thanksgiving, a tragic school-bus accident killed many local children. The museum volunteer on duty, surprised that we hadn't heard of the tragedy, quietly led us through a scrapbook of the newspaper articles documenting the rescue efforts. Less tragic, but just as meaningful, is the knickknack-filled display case just past a slab 5 feet in diameter taken from a tree said to have been the largest pine tree in the area. While the case contains some valuable glass and porcelain antiques, it also holds a wind-up plastic penguin, a yellow rubber lizard, and a small, well-used pincushion. One visitor laughed and said it should be called "Things we keep on our kitchen windowsills." A museum volunteer responded that indeed, for many families, keeping a loved one's item on the windowsill is what keeps the memory of that person most alive.

Lake Chelan Historical Museum • 204 E Woodin Avenue, Chelan, Washington 98816 • (509) 682-5644

Admission: By donation. **Hours:** June–Sept: Mon–Sat 1pm–4pm. **To get there:** The museum is at the corner of Woodin Avenue and Emerson Street in downtown Chelan.

Dial 'O' for Operator

CLE ELUM
Cle Elum Historical Telephone Museum

This regional museum takes special pride in promoting its unique role in the history of Northwest telephone technology. Housed in the town's old telephone office building, the museum commemorates and celebrates the fact that on September 18, 1966, Cle Elum was the last place in the Pacific Northwest to switch over from operator-assisted phone calls to automatic direct dial.

Cle Elum got its first telephones in 1901. To make a phone call, residents had to turn a crank on their telephone at home. This made a small numbered tab drop at the central telephone switchboard and signaled one of the two town operators to plug in her cord and help complete the call. During the years when few people had phones and nearly everyone knew one another, callers rarely used a telephone directory or asked for a particular telephone number. They'd just tell the operator who they were looking for, and if that person wasn't at home, the operator would often know where they were. When the area was bustling with mining activity, it was crucial that operators understood several languages, because people of more than 25 nationalities had flocked to Cle Elum to work in the mines.

The museum displays the three increasingly sophisticated telephone switchboards used between 1901 and 1966. One is especially long, and a retired local operator remembers using a fishing rod to help her reach its far tabs. There's an array of telephone-wire insulators in a wide assortment of shapes and colors, the town's first printed telephone directory, a progression of telephones from early black crank models through pink push-button styles, and the plugs, switches, and cords that operators used to connect callers. There's also a calculagraph, an early device used to track long-distance phone calls.

While the museum celebrates the important role operators played in keeping a town connected, it does not formally recognize the unique bill collection service that such operator-staffed phone systems provided. One woman who was a Cle Elum operator for more than 24 years remembers one occasion when a man tried to drive away from the pay telephone located just outside the telephone building, without waiting for the operator to ring back with the amount due for his long distance phone call. The operator on duty simply opened the window, leaned out, and yelled, "Excuse me, sir— I'm taking down your license plate number." The bill was paid.

Cle Elum Historical Telephone Museum • 221 E 1st Street, Cle Elum, Washington 98922 • (509) 674-5702
Admission: Free. Hours: Memorial Day–Labor Day: Mon–Fri 10am–4pm, Sat–Sun 12pm–4pm; best to call ahead. To get there: The museum is at the corner of E 1st and Wright avenues in downtown Cle Elum.

Train-Lovers' Haven

CLE ELUM
The Moore House

South of the town of Cle Elum is the Moore House, a bed-and-breakfast that was built in 1909 as a bunkhouse for workers of the Chicago, Milwaukee, St. Paul and Pacific Railroad, which ran through the area. According to Eric and Cindy Sherwood, who now operate the B&B, overnight guests sometimes include retired railroad workers who once bunked here on the job.

The Sherwoods have amassed quite a collection of CM & STP Railroad and other railroad memorabilia, including china and menus from dining cars, linen, blankets and pillowcases from sleeper cars, a full conductor's uniform, photos, railroad postcards, matchbooks, timetables, and more. Most of it is displayed in glass cases lining the hallway, but there's more in the guest rooms, each named after a railroad crewman who actually stayed at the bunk-house. You don't need to be a guest here to view the collection. The best time to visit is in the afternoon, when the rooms are empty.

The Moore House • PO Box 629, South Cle Elum, Washington 98943 • (509) 674-5939
Admission: Free. **Hours:** By appointment only. **To get there:** Take the Cle Elum/South Cle Elum exit off I-90. Turn right at Rosetti Street (the South Cle Elum turnoff) and go down a short hill to a stop sign. Go straight, under the I-90 over-pass, and over the Yakima River. Turn right at Madison Street. Go two blocks to the stop sign and turn left. Continue four blocks; the Moore House is at the bend in the road.

One Outlaw's Bad End

DAVENPORT
Lincoln County
Historical Museum

D avenport promotes itself as a "darn nice place to visit," and the Lincoln County Historical Museum is a darn nice place in which to spend a few hours learning about the area's agri-cultural and cultural history. While the museum is well-known for its shed full of farm machinery, steam engines, and covered wag-ons, most visitors are morbidly drawn to the museum's Harry Tracy display.

Tracy was a Wisconsin-born kid who came West and turned to a life of crime, allegedly hanging out for a while with the Hole in the Wall Gang. In 1899 he hooked up with David Merrill and together they committed a string of robberies and holdups in the Portland area, gaining notoriety as the Black Mackinaw Bandits be-cause they wore long black raincoats "on the job." The pair was arrested and jailed at the Oregon State Penitentiary in Salem, but

Outlaw Harry Tracy ran from the law one too many times.

they broke out in June of 1902, killing several guards in the process. While on the run, Tracy killed his friend Merrill and some policemen in Seattle, boasting openly about his escapades as he evaded capture throughout the Northwest.

By August, Tracy had made his way to the Eddy Ranch in eastern Washington's wheat country. When a five-man posse from nearby Creston came after him, Tracy headed for cover in an unharvested wheatfield, but not before getting shot and wounded in one leg. A short while later the posse heard a rifle shot from somewhere in the field. Afraid to wade in after the outlaw, the small posse stood guard overnight waiting for backups. In the morning Tracy's body was found just 200 yards from the edge of the field. He had shot himself rather than surrender or be captured.

Tracy artifacts on display here include a plaster death mask, a frying pan he used while on the run, and a bullet from his cartridge belt. Photographs and books about his life are for sale in the gift shop.

Most of the other exhibits are less gruesome. The museum
has a meteor discovered in Egypt, a town about 20 miles north of
Davenport, and a photo gallery of area farms, schools, and early
town buildings. Look carefully at the cases near the re-created general store downstairs, just to the right of the entrance. You'll see
14 neatly framed used sparkplugs.

**Lincoln County Historical Museum • PO Box 869, Davenport,
Washington 99122 • (509) 725-6711**
Admission: Free. **Hours:** May–Sept: Mon–Sat 9am–5pm, Sun 1pm–5pm; other
times by appointment. **To get there:** The museum is located just off Route 2, at
the intersection of Park and 7th.

Avoiding the Big Bang

DUPONT
DuPont Historical Museum

In 1906 the E. I. du Pont de Nemours & Co. chemical firm
bought 5 square miles of land surrounding Fort Nisqually, south
of Tacoma. The seller was Edward Huggins, the last representative of the Hudson's Bay Co., which had operated the trading
post at the fort. The new owners built a dynamite factory, and the
company town of DuPont came into existence. In the years that
followed, virtually all of DuPont's male population, and some of
the women, worked at the factory. The village of 400 people
boasted a church, a school, two stores, a clubhouse, a hotel, and
a butcher shop. The butcher shop later served as City Hall, and
this tiny wooden building is now the home of the DuPont Historical Museum.

The collection includes a number of interesting artifacts from
the days when Hudson's Bay reigned supreme, including a brick
from the SS *Beaver*, a Hudson's Bay boat that was the first

steamship to ply the Pacific. But the museum's jewel—a collection of photos and memorabilia detailing the making of dynamite and the history of the town—is in the back room.

There's a Starrett gelatin packing machine (used to mix and press the dynamite into sticks), samples of the shell paper in which the sticks were wrapped, and honeycombed wooden boxes used for shipping the dynamite.

DuPont workers, as a mannequin shows, wore cotton uniforms with no metal parts. They used tools such as wooden shovels and non-sparking welding torches. Vigilant guards kept even a single match from entering the premises.

But despite these precautions, there were plenty of accidents. The volunteer who showed us around, Nina Ogrin, grew up in DuPont. Her father helped build the factory and later worked in its acid department; nearly every other member of her family also worked there at one time or another. "Oh, there were lots of explosions. Quite a few where the men were killed, too. Our neighbor lost his arm. The worst part was when the other men had to come in after an explosion and pick up the pieces, which wasn't very pleasant."

The plant finally shut down in the mid-1970s, and nearly all of the village's current 600 residents are retired DuPont employees or their family members. Most of the others in DuPont work at one of the two nearby military bases, Fort Lewis and McChord Air Force Base. The land is now owned by the Weyerhaeuser Co. and is scheduled for development.

DuPont Historical Museum • 207 Barksdale Avenue, DuPont, Washington 98327 • (206) 964-2399
Admission: Free. **Hours:** Sept–Apr: Sun 1pm–4pm; May–Aug: also open Wed 7pm–9pm • **To get there:** Take exit 119 off I-5. Follow the signs to DuPont, which is just off the freeway. Barksdale Avenue is DuPont's main street; the museum is a small white wooden building on the right.

Front-Yard Art

Dick and Jane's Spot

Dick Elliott and Jane Orleman are artists who came to Ellensburg to attend college and ended up settling here. In the late 1970s, they bought an old frame house at the corner of First and Pearl and began to decorate its exterior, as well as the front and back yards and the surrounding fence, with art— colorful bits of "found" art and pieces of their own making. Various friends got into the act, Elliott and Orleman added pieces purchased from other artists, and eventually their house became Ellensburg's premier roadside attraction: Dick and Jane's Spot.

A multicolored kiosk on the side of the house explains what the heck is going on, and there's a guestbook to sign (Jane says that during the summer about 100 people a week write in it). A sign on the kiosk also requests that visitors not enter the grounds but restrict their viewing to what is visible from the street. The forbidden garden—especially the backyard, in which you can just glimpse eccentric brick fountains and wild chairs among the vegetables and flowers—is surely tempting; but there's plenty to see just from the street.

Kinetic sculptures, made by Dick from bicycle wheels and safety reflectors, catch the breeze and sunlight and make a very satisfying and colorful commotion. Chief among Jane's contributions are wonderfully funky mannequins that gesture from the front yard. Richard Beyer, who created the popular *People Waiting for the Interurban* in Seattle, has a bear sculpture in the front yard. The bear holds several human heads, which Jane says represent the Seattle Arts Commission.

A gigantic white hand—a relic from a retired fortune-teller's studio that friends salvaged and brought to the Spot—hangs from the second floor. And all around are strange bits of found and/or created things, ranging in materials from Prince Albert tobacco tins to ceramic telephone-wire insulators. Jane estimates that visitors can see the work of some 35 artists from the street—and the collection is always changing.

Dick and Jane's Spot • 101 N Pearl Street, Ellensburg, Washington 98926
Admission: Free. Hours: Open for outdoor viewing anytime; don't forget, this is a private home. To get there: The house is on the corner of 1st and Pearl, across the street from the police station.

The Largest Building in the World

The Boeing Co., Everett Plant

The sights seen on the Boeing Co. tour of its Everett plant, where 747s and 767s are assembled and finished, are mind-bendingly big. The main building is the world's largest structure by volume—a 60-acre behemoth so vast that your eyes and brain have a hard time comprehending it. Seen from the catwalk above the assembly area, a network of 20 overhead cranes, each with a 34-ton capacity, hefts cargo containers with ease; below, a chattering circus of workers rivet and weld and seal the skins of the huge airplanes. At the same time, tiny details are visible: people ride bicycles—old-fashioned ones with touring handlebars—from one corner of the building to another. The tops of toolboxes are decorated with photos of girlfriends, wives, and children. A trio of workers is on break, eating sandwiches and reading the morning paper at a desk.

Boeing's tour guides are walking encyclopedias. The 60-acre building is equal to five and a half Kingdomes, or nearly 60 football fields. Twenty thousand people work here, around the clock, turning out ten jet aircraft a month. By 1994 the building will have expanded, covering nearly 100 acres, to accommodate Boeing's new line of 777s. Fifty percent of each 747 is made by Boeing in the Seattle area; the rest is subcontracted worldwide. A single 747 goes for $130 million to $158 million, depending on options. Each one has 6 million parts. When an airplane is painted (which takes place in a separate building), the paint alone adds 800 pounds to the plane's weight. But perhaps the most interesting detail about the world's largest building is this: it has no heating or air conditioning facilities. Though the heat generated by workers and machinery is sufficient in winter, there are complaints from workers about hot summer temperatures.

The recorded message about the tour gives instructions on reaching the site and other information. Tours run Monday through Friday, about every half hour, in morning and afternoon shifts. Children under the age of 10 are not allowed (for insurance purposes). A walk of about one-third of a mile (along an underground facilities tunnel) is necessary. You must climb up and down a set of stairs at the beginning and end of the tour. Cameras, video

cameras, and backpacks are strictly forbidden (if you show up in line with one, you'll have to take it back to your car). The tour lasts about one hour, with an optional half-hour film available.

Here are some other things to bear in mind: The tour is a popular attraction, and even in the non-tourist seasons, you should be prepared to wait (only 45 people are allowed on a given tour, and slots fill up fast; in addition, some places are reserved by organized tour groups). There is no place to sit down if you want to keep your place in line. Try to find a bathroom before you line up; once you're in line, you'll find no facilities until the tour is over. The catwalk (reached by way of a freight elevator) is very high, and the far corners of the building very distant, so bring a pair of binoculars.

The Boeing Co., Everett Plant • 3003 W Casino Road, Paine Field, Everett, Washington 98203 • (206) 342-4801 or (206) 655-1131 (from Seattle)
Admission: Free. Hours: Mon–Fri 9am–11:30am and 1pm–3:30pm. **To get there:** From I-5, take exit 189 and go west 3½ miles on Highway 526. Take the Tour Center exit and follow the signs.

Whale Songs

FRIDAY HARBOR
The Whale Museum

I f you're not lucky enough to see real whales on your ferry ride to San Juan Island, or if you just want to find out more about these huge mammals, stop by the Whale Museum.

Sea-green steps, a whale mural, and a haunting recording of whale songs bring you up to the museum entrance and get you in the mood for learning more about these mysterious and wonderful ocean creatures. The museum's goal is to educate the public about the marine environment, "especially its mammalian inhabitants." Here you'll learn (or be reminded) that whales aren't giant fish, but intelligent, warm-blooded, air-breathing mammals. Orcas, the large black-and-white animals known commonly as "killer whales," are members of the family of toothed whales and are closely related to dolphins.

For a little perspective on just how big whales are, stand near one of the whale skeletons in the museum. Try the 8-month-old gray-whale calf skeleton hanging from the ceiling, more than 24 feet long; the whale probably weighed 2½ tons. Or stand near the 14-foot, life-size model of a newborn humpback whale, or imagine coming across the skeleton of a minke whale calf found washed up on the shore of San Juan Island.

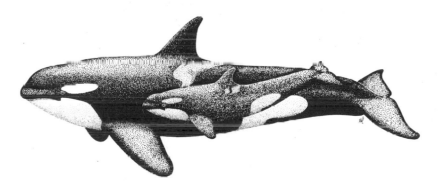

The museum is extremely child-friendly throughout, and there is a special children's room with whale puzzles, windows looking out over the water, crayons, and books about the ocean for young readers. In the quiet, well-stocked library corner there's an old-time radio. Switch it on and you'll hear an edition of "Whale News" from a Bellevue high school radio station. There's also a phone booth set up at one end of the museum, but it's not for making calls. Instead, visitors are invited to step inside, close the door, lift the receiver, and listen to the sounds of bow-head whales, bearded seals, beluga whales, and walruses. All were recorded beneath the Arctic ice and are somehow both eerie and soothing.

The education lesson continues in the well-stocked gift shop, where a case labeled "not for sale" has items confiscated under the Marine Mammal Protection Act: walrus tusks, ivory, whale teeth, turtle bracelets, sealskin toys, and moisturizing cream made with spermaceti, a waxy substance that comes from whale oil.

The Whale Museum • 62 1st Street N, Friday Harbor, Washington 98250 • (206) 378-4710
Admission: $3 for adults, discounts for children and senior citizens. Hours: Memorial Day–Sept: every day 10am–5pm; Oct–May: every day 11am–4pm. To get there: The museum is located on the second floor of a white clapboard building on 1st Street N, just a short (uphill) walk from the ferry landing in Friday Harbor.

The Night Sky

GOLDENDALE
Goldendale Observatory

The Goldendale Observatory boasts the nation's largest amateur-built telescope of its kind that is available full-time for public viewing. The telescope is a 24½-inch reflecting Cassegrain built by four Vancouver, Washington, men and situated under the clear skies of Goldendale. The facility, which is operated by the Washington State Parks and Recreation Commission, can be booked overnight by qualified "serious amateurs" who have passed an oral exam given by the resident ranger. A resource library is also available to serious amateurs.

Goldendale Observatory • 1602 Observatory Drive, Goldendale, Washington 98620 • (509) 773-3141
Admission: Free. **Hours:** Apr–Sept: Wed–Sun 2pm–5pm and 8pm–12am; Oct–Mar: Sat 1pm–5pm and 7pm–9pm, Sun 1pm–5pm; other times by appointment. **To get there:** The observatory is a few miles outside Goldendale. Go east on 142 and north on 97. Follow the signs.

French Fashion Mannequins

Maryhill Museum

At the turn of the century, railroad man, lawyer, entrepreneur, and international *bon vivant* Sam Hill bought 7,000 acres in the desolate, remote Columbia River Gorge country. His intent was to build both a Quaker farming community and a lavish home for himself. Construction of Sam Hill's mansion, a 50-foot-high French chateau–style structure of poured concrete, began in 1914 on a remote bluff south of Goldendale with spectacular views of the Columbia Gorge. By calling his project "Maryhill," he cannily honored his wife, daughter, and mother-in-law in a single stroke.

But Hill's grand vision failed; his wife returned East without ever visiting the house. Hill's planned utopian community likewise never took shape. His half-finished house lay dormant during the First World War, until Hill's close friend Loie Fuller, a modern dancer with ties to the Parisian art scene, urged him to turn it into a museum.

Loie Fuller was one of three women who figured largely in Maryhill's development as a museum. After the First World War, when he had been active in raising funds for European relief, Hill had befriended Queen Marie of Romania. In 1926 he invited her

29

to travel to his remote corner of the world for the museum's dedication. She accepted the invitation, becoming the first queen ever to visit the United States, and arrived by train in a highly publicized tour. The museum, however, was still an empty shell. A third friend of Hill's, San Francisco sugar heiress Alma Spreckels, assumed responsibility for the museum's completion after his death in 1931. Maryhill officially opened in 1940.

Sam Hill's story is astonishing. The Maryhill story is astonishing. The building itself is astonishing. But what is inside is also astonishing. Who would expect a collection like Maryhill's in the stark setting of the Columbia Gorge, in a mock-European park complete with peacocks?

The permanent collections at Maryhill have roughly equal measures of importance, charm, and eccentricity. Loie Fuller's contacts in Paris helped Hill acquire a collection of sculptures and drawings by Auguste Rodin, as well as other works of French art. An extensive chess collection includes ancient Chinese sets, modern Israeli pieces, huge wooden chessmen from 18th-century Spain, and spiked Persian sets for playing chess on sand or cushions. A large collection of Native American artifacts features prehistoric rock carvings, baskets, and beadwork. And the Queen Marie Gallery displays heavy wooden gilt furniture, jewelry, Russian icons, and other royal memorabilia, including the gown Her Majesty wore to the coronation of Czar Nicholas II.

But perhaps most interesting is Maryhill's collection of French fashion mannequins. In the aftermath of the Second World War, the once-dominant French fashion industry was in ruins. It lacked even the most rudimentary supplies of materials with which to create new styles. In 1945 the Chambre Syndicale de la Couture Parisienne (the official organization of top Parisian designers) decided to assemble an extraordinary road show, Théâtre de la Mode.

A young sculptor, Eliane Bonabel, was commissioned to create a series of mannequins, each one-third normal human size, from thin wire armature. All the major Parisian designers—including Balenciaga, Schiaparelli, Worth, Lanvin, and Ricci—created

miniature fashions for these dolls. Top jewelers, coiffeurs, and accessories designers were brought in. Several distinguished visual artists, including Jean Cocteau, created backdrops and sets. Special music was composed to accompany them.

The mannequins went on a world tour and were a great success, helping to revive the fortunes of the French fashion industry and to raise money for the relief organization Entr'Aide Française. But by the time their final show came—at the City of Paris department store in San Francisco—no one wanted them. Alma Spreckels, a major arts patron in San Francisco and the trustee of Maryhill, arranged for some 158 mannequins and a portion of the original garments and accessories to be donated to the museum. There they remained, largely unnoticed and in disrepair, until they were "discovered" by Stanley Garfinkel, an assistant professor of history at Kent State University, while preparing a documentary on designer Christian Dior. Garfinkel helped arrange for the mannequins' restoration in Paris in the late 1980s, and they are now back at Maryhill in their full glory. The stage sets have been re-created as closely as possible to the originals, the dresses have been cleaned and restored, and the accessories shine.

Maryhill Museum of Art • 35 Maryhill Museum Drive, Goldendale, Washington 98620 • (509) 773-3733
Admission: $4 for adults, discounts for children. **Hours:** Mar 15–Nov 15: every day 9am–5pm. **To get there:** The museum is on Highway 97, about 8 miles south of Goldendale. Follow the signs; it's hard to miss.

A Native American Perspective

Colville Confederated Tribes Museum

While many county historical museums proudly display their collections of Native American artifacts, the focus is usually on pioneer families who settled the land that native people already called home. We felt a sharp difference in perspective when we stepped into the two exhibit showrooms at the Colville Confederated Tribes Museum, just down the street from Grand Coulee Dam.

The main room features murals painted by tribe members in 1989, depicting fishing scenes and the Kettle Falls fishing grounds as they might have looked 150 years ago. Okanogan tribal elder and museum director Andy Joseph told us that, for tribal members, "the most treasured part of the museum is the collection of photographs of what our people looked like." These pictures, dating back to the 1870s, are the only ancestral images many tribal members have ever seen. There are also life-size dioramas showing fishing, gambling, and sweat-lodge activities, and a tepee made of tule reed gathered by a sixth-grade class. Reed tepees were popular because the reeds would shrink in the summer, allowing air

Chief Sarsarpikin, also known as Chief Avalanche,
of the Okanogan tribe in 1883.

to circulate, and swell again in the winter, keeping water out. Andy
Joseph is present most of the time during regular hours, and is
more than willing to tell you stories about the items on display and
about Colville traditions.

**Colville Confederated Tribes Museum • 526 Birch Street, PO Box
233, Coulee Dam, Washington 99116 • (509) 633-0751**
Admission: By donation. **Hours:** Mon–Fri 8am–5pm. **To get there:** From the visitor center and the dam, follow Route 155 (Columbia Avenue) across the river and
onto Roosevelt Way. Turn left at the tepee, onto Birch Street. The museum is on
your left.

Spinning Chamber Pots

GRAND COULEE/COULEE DAM/COULEE CITY
Gehrke Windmill Garden

The fame and awe-inspiring mass of Grand Coulee Dam sadly overshadow another great man-made wonder, the Gehrke Windmill Garden. Emil Gehrke, an ironworker and millwright from Nebraska who lived in Grand Coulee for 21 years, made these remarkable folk-art windmills out of what most of us would call junk. He estimates that he and his wife, Vera, traveled 62,000 miles by car over the years to collect materials. (Vera also painted every windmill by hand.)

The 100-plus working windmills spinning here are brightly painted constructions made of plastic bowling pins, hard hats, Jell-O molds, chandeliers, hubcaps, pieces of farm machinery, and bicycle wheels. Our favorite was a coffeepot ringed by spinning coffee cups. A number of the Gehrkes' windmills are also part of an outdoor art exhibit at the Viewlands/Hoffman electrical substation at 145th and Fremont Avenue N in Seattle.

Gehrke Windmill Garden • North Dam Rest Area, Grand Coulee
Hours: Daylight. **To get there:** The garden is in the North Dam Rest Area on SR 155 as you enter the town of Grand Coulee.

Eighth Wonder of the World

GRAND COULEE/COULEE DAM/COULEE CITY
Grand Coulee Dam

No visit to this area is complete without a stop at Grand Coulee Dam. Built in the 1930s and dedicated in 1941, the dam is the largest producer of electricity in the United States

President Franklin D. Roosevelt surveys the dam's progress in 1937.

and the third-largest in the world, after the Guri Dam in Venezuela and Itaipu Dam between Paraguay and Brazil. You can picnic beside it, meander through the visitor center, or tour the dam's pump generator and power plants.

Whether you tour alone or in the company of a friendly, fact-filled Bureau of Land Reclamation guide, you're sure to want to know the answer to these most-asked questions:

Which dam is larger, Grand Coulee or Hoover? (Grand Coulee, with 12 million cubic yards of concrete to Hoover's mere 4.4 million, has more volume—but Hoover Dam, at 726 feet, is 176 feet taller than Grand Coulee.)

And just how much *is* 12 million cubic yards of concrete? (Enough, says the bureau's handy flier, to build a 4-foot-wide, 4-inch-thick sidewalk 50,000 miles long, or twice around the equator.)

Armed with these facts and wanting to learn more, we climbed aboard the 50-passenger glass elevator that descends to the dam's third powerhouse. Most kids love the ride, but we admit to being a little nervous on the way down, despite the guide's assurances that—contrary to popular rumors—nobody is buried in the dam.

Grand Coulee Dam • Grand Coulee, Washington 99133 • (509) 633-9265
Admission: Free. **Hours:** (Visitor Center) Oct 1–Memorial Day: every day 9am–5pm; June–July: every day 8:30am–11pm; August: every day 8:30am–10:30pm; Sept: every day 8:30am–9:30pm. **To get there:** From Grand Coulee, take SR 155 north and follow the signs to the dam's visitor center.

Faithful Mascot

GRAND COULEE/COULEE DAM/COULEE CITY
Coulee Dam Mini-Museum

In the basement of Coulee City's City Hall is a Coulee Dam Mini-Museum that features dam artifacts and photographs of the dam construction. Ask for the key to this room at the City Hall Municipal Office, Room 111. A scrapbook of newspaper clippings documents the dam project from beginning to end, and the Coulee City high school mascot—a stuffed beaver—presides over the room. Schools in the area used to take turns stealing it from one another, and although no one at City Hall on the day we visited could tell us why it is in the museum, we like to think that some savvy schoolteacher brought it here for safekeeping.

Coulee Dam Mini-Museum • City Hall, 300 Lincoln, Coulee City, Washington 99116 • (509) 633-0320
Admission: Free. **Hours:** Mon–Fri 9am–5pm. **To get there:** Follow Route 155 (it turns into Columbia Drive) down the hill past the dam into Coulee City. Take a left at Douglas Street and go up the hill two blocks to a large white building. That's City Hall.

Picking and Plucking

Furford Cranberry Museum

Cape Cod isn't the only place with the right mix of sea climate and peat bogs to constitute perfect cranberry country. People around Grayland have been farming cranberries since 1915, and the area provides a large percentage of America's Thanksgiving cranberries and cranberry-based juices.

At the Furford Cranberry Museum you'll learn about how cranberries have been harvested and processed over the years. Until the 1940s they were picked by hand. Pickers would simply get down on their hands and knees, pluck the berries, and put them into a big box. A good picker could fill up to ten boxes a day. Later, one- and two-handed cranberry scoops sped up the process, and by the early 1950s there was even a suction picker. But it was a cranberry farmer with a sore back who really revolutionized cranberry picking.

In 1956 Julius Furford invented a practical automated cranberry picker. According to shop manager and museum guide Clyde Mears, "people had their doubts, but they watched him, and he was done picking in no time." Furford's invention is a motor driven machine with combs, or shoes, on the bottom that pick up the cranberry vine and pluck the cranberries off as it moves through a field. What's more, it prunes the vines while harvesting the berries. Furford went into business manufacturing and selling his machines. Now in his eighties, he "isn't poor," says Mears, and he still works and still invents. He's often at the museum on Saturdays, but if he's not around, ask a museum staffer to play the descriptive video Furford narrates that shows cranberry pickers in action, with and without the Furford picker.

Before you leave, be sure to stop at the museum snack bar. Complimentary coffee is always brewing, and you'll get a free sample of Mrs. Mears's award-winning cranberry fudge.

Furford Cranberry Museum • Highway 105 N, Route 1, Box 111, Grayland, Washington 98547 • (206) 267-3303 (weekdays) or (206) 267-7314 (weekends)

Admission: Free. **Hours:** Summer: Sat–Sun 10am–5pm; closed Dec–Feb; other times by appointment. **To get there:** The museum is located in a building behind Furford's manufacturing plant. Look for a small sign on the left-hand side of the road as you drive north on Highway 105 towards Grayland. It looks as if you're in the wrong place, but you're not.

Running by the Tides

ILWACO
Ilwaco Heritage Museum

Museum volunteer Tenho Harju grew up in Ilwaco, and if you really want to know what's what in this museum, be sure to ask if he's around to give you a guided tour.

Harju told us about the traditions and lifestyle of the Chinook Indians, and about how the local cranberry industry won the area the title "Cape Cod of the West." He demonstrated the use of an old-time salmon trap and said, "It worked so well that it was later outlawed." He showed us the old post office desk made from packing crates used in the salmon cannery and, with a wink, told us that the cannery night watchman made it a long time ago for the postmistress, whom he hoped to woo with his handiwork. Upstairs we marveled at the 7-foot-tall, turquoise-encrusted carved wooden Indian that weighs 300 pounds, and peeked inside every window in the miniature dollhouses, where miniature families were getting ready for Christmas. Then we set out for the Ilwaco Railroad Depot building out back.

The Ilwaco Railroad and Navigation Company, also known as the Clamshell Railroad, served the towns along Washington's Long Beach Peninsula from 1889 until 1930. The railroad had a reputation for being somewhat irregular, because in order to meet the river steamers at either end of the line, it had adjusted its schedule to the tides. The depot is all that's left of the railroad; it was moved to the museum lot for restoration by the members of the Ilwaco Railroad and Navigation Company Model Club. Inside the depot they built a 50-foot-long model of Long Beach Peninsula as it looked around 1920, complete with miniature railroad and buildings made to scale out of cereal boxes and old lottery tickets.

Ilwaco Heritage Museum • 115 SE Lake Street, PO Box 153, Ilwaco, Washington 98624 • (206) 642-3446
Admission: $1.50 for adults, discounts for children and senior citizens. **Hours:** Mon–Sat 9am–5pm, Sun 12pm–4pm. **To get there:** Going north on US 101 turn left on Williams Avenue, then take a right on Lake Street. The museum is also the Ilwaco Convention Center, and that sign is more visible than the museum's.

Chez Jake

LONG BEACH
Marsh's Free Museum

ravel in the American South, and all roads lead to the North Carolina tourist mecca known as South of the Border. Go anywhere near South Dakota and you'll surely end up at Wall Drug. Visit Washington's Long Beach Peninsula and you'll find yourself mysteriously drawn to Marsh's Free Museum, home of Jake the Alligator Man. It's a faded wood building with a low porch cluttered with giant carved wooden cowboys and Indians, old pig-scalding kettles, and assorted farm equipment.

In the same way that Jake is supposedly half man–half alligator, Marsh's is half museum–half souvenir shop. You can buy the T-shirts and saltwater taffy, but the shrunken head from South America is for viewing only; it sits in a glass box, on top of an antique coin-operated scale and below a stuffed bison head.

Jake, the star attraction, is way back in the far corner, past the case that invites you to insert a dime so the "imported French canary" inside will sing, and past the "Throne of Love," which, for another coin, will test your passion. The place has the aura of a sideshow, but look slowly and carefully and you'll discover some neat stuff: an example of the world's first mousetrap, a really old ice-cube maker, turn-of-the-century valentines and vacuum cleaners, and a llama-tooth necklace.

Shelves near the front door are lined with preserved and

stuffed animals, including a two-headed pig. As we were leaving the shop a visitor came in and marveled that the cat lounging on the front counter was exactly where he'd seen it last year. "No," said the woman at the cash register, "the cat you saw last year died. We freeze-dried him and put him up on that shelf over there. This kitty showed up a few days later. He looks just like our old cat, and hangs out in the same spot."

Watch out, kitty.

Marsh's Free Museum • Pacific Highway 103, Long Beach, Washington 98631 • (206) 642-2188
Admission: Free. **Hours:** Summer: every day 9am–10pm; winter: every day 9am–6pm. **To get there:** Head north on US 103. Marsh's is on your left as you enter downtown Long Beach.

The Story of Kites

LONG BEACH
World Kite Museum and Hall of Fame

K ite fliers, especially those who like to fly really big kites, love Long Beach because there's lots of wind and 28 miles of beach uninterrupted by electrical wires, telephone poles, or other things that can get in the way of a successful flight. The annual kite festival here draws hundreds of kite fliers and thousands of spectators from around the world each August. Each year the festival organizers aim to break the western hemisphere record for the most kites in the sky at one time.

The World Kite Museum and Hall of Fame opened in 1990 and already has more than 600 kites representing 14 countries and 31 states, as well as a growing collection of kite books and colorful pictures of kites in flight, including a photo of the largest kite in the world. When the 550-square-meter kite flew at Long Beach, it took 17 people to carry it to the field, and more than 60 to hold the lines to keep it from flying away.

Here there are miniature kites no bigger than a matchbox and gifts from visiting kite teams, such as the all-white kite presented by the Thai Heritage Kite Team. There are bird kites and box kites, stunt kites, six- and seven-sided flat kites, and more.

Take the time to read about the history of kites and their role in transportation, rescue efforts, and mail delivery. During the Second World War, kites with pictures of enemy airplanes

Frenchman Arthur Batut pioneered aerial photography in the 1880s by sending a camera aloft in a kite.

emblazoned on them were used as targets by gunners in training, and box kites were standard equipment in lifeboats. They helped to lift an aerial so a rescue signal could be transmitted.

The Kite Museum's Hall of Fame honors famous kite fliers (including Benjamin Franklin) and kite inventors, and also introduces visitors to the Father of Aerophotography, Arthur Batut. In the late 1880s this French photographer watched a butterfly floating by with its wings perfectly still. Imagining what a great aerial snapshot that butterfly could take if it had a camera, Batut decided to send his camera aloft in a kite. He couldn't click the shutter by remote control, so he sent a small burning wick along for the ride. When the wick burned down, the shutter clicked, and voilà! an aerophotograph.

World Kite Museum and Hall of Fame • 104 Pacific Avenue N, PO Box 964, Long Beach, Washington 98631 • (206) 642-4020
Admission: $1 for adults, discounts for children and senior citizens. **Hours:** June–Aug: Fri–Mon 11am–5pm; Sept–May: Sat–Sun 11am–4pm; other times by appointment. **To get there:** Take Pacific Highway 103 north to Long Beach. After the traffic light, take the second left, onto 3rd Street NW. The museum is on your right.

From Horse Carriage to Horsepower

LYNDEN
Transportation Collection, Lynden Historical Museum

One of the best collections of antique vehicles in the Northwest is available for viewing in Lynden, a pleasant farming town near the Canadian border. A local farmer and horse breeder, Fred K. Polander, donated his collection of horse-drawn carriages to the city, and curator George Young, a retired border patrolman, has worked hard to maintain and supplement it. Among the 50 horse-drawn carriages on display are a black Victoria cab with ornate glass lamps; a "rubberneck wagon" that was used for sightseeing at Yellowstone, Rainier, and McKinley national parks; two ornate miniature Viceroy carts, used for showing fancy dress horses; vintage wagons used for delivering milk and dry cleaning ("Pacific Laundry, Phone 126 Bellingham"); and a cart with a cleverly concealed rumble seat.

The automobile section includes a wonderful cream-colored 1937 Fiat Topolino ("Little Mouse") with delightful art deco curves. There's a 1925 sedan done up for winter driving, with side curtains, a cover for the radiator, and chains on the rear wheels. A dozen old Chevies show the evolution of that make; they include the 15th wood-bodied Chevy truck ever made, a rare center-door model, and a 1920 black sedan with every extra you can think of. The collection is rounded out with such items as old gas and tire advertisements, huge gangstermobiles from the 1930s, and a "bone-crusher"–style bicycle (the sort with an oversized front wheel), made for the mayor of Lynden by his blacksmith father. "The mayor can ride it real well," Young says.

The museum has many other displays, perhaps the most arresting being a series of miniature scenes re-creating aspects of Nazi acts of terrorism. One tabletop-sized tableau details a rally in a Bavarian village square, complete with marching band, tanks, dignitaries on a dais, and dozens of saluting soldiers. Young says: "This was done by a local guy who went to work and just got carried away with himself. I kind of wish he'd chosen a different subject matter, but you've got to admire the detail."

Lynden Historical Museum • 217 W Front Street, Lynden, Washington 98264 • (206) 354-3675

Admission: $2 for adults, discounts for senior citizens. Hours: Apr–Oct: Mon–Sat 10am–5pm; Nov–Mar: Wed–Sat 10am–4pm. To get there: From I-5, take the Lynden exit to Guide Meridian. Head north to the Lynden cutoff; the road becomes Front Street.

You Don't Want to Know...

MONROE
Antique Medical Instruments, Valley General Hospital

In 1920, Dr. Minard Allison came to Monroe and bought the practice of a retiring general practitioner. After Allison's death, a number of his instruments were donated to the local historical society. The society also has a large collection of antique medical instruments donated in the 1980s by the Department of Medical History and Ethics of the University of Washington. The less scary of these items are on display in the lobby of Monroe's Valley General Hospital. The rest can be seen by appointment at the historical society, but they are not for the squeamish.

The items in the hospital lobby include examples and descriptions of such turn-of-the-century remedies as turpentine for hemorrhaging, ergot of rye to stimulate contractions, iron and arsenic to build red blood corpuscles (the box is labeled "Poison—Sugar-Coated"), and opium for pain relief. There are also such antique pediatric tools as a wooden fetuscope (for listening to a prenatal heartbeat) and an old-fashioned baby bottle with its identifying carton: "Grip-Tight Miniature Feeder."

Other displays feature an amputation saw, a pair of medical saddlebags from the 1890s, and a collection of vintage prescriptions. There's also a fascinating look at home remedies, with containers, drawings, and descriptions of such herbs as tansy, skullcap, comfrey, and yarrow. A line drawing and text, reproduced from a turn-of-the-century book, details the making of "a pork and onion poultice . . . good for wounds made by rusty tools or nails, bruises, and lacerated wounds."

Among the items at the museum are an Albee Electro-Operative Bone Set for orthopedic surgery; a wooden examination

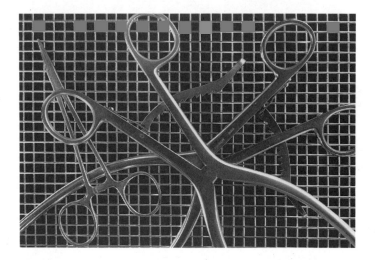

table with ingeniously built tilting table and stirrups; a pre–Second World War Army Medical Corps EKG machine; containers of obsolete medications such as "Castex Rigid Bandage" and "Vapo-Cresolene"; a blue-and-white-enameled female urinal; and a terrifying 6-foot steel rack holding a set of giant glass nipples with red rubber tubing coming out of their bottoms. A tiny plaque on the rack's base reads: "Colonic Mobile Unit." Volunteer Doris Reiner says, "I never look at that thing without thinking, 'Boy, I'm glad medical science has advanced.'"

Monroe Historical Society • 218 E Main Street, Monroe, Washington 98272 • (206) 794-5488
Admission: By donation. **Hours:** Open by appointment. **To get there:** From I-5, take Highway 2 east to Monroe. Turn east at the stoplight in the center of town. The museum is in the old firehouse.

Valley General Hospital • 14701 179th Avenue SE, Monroe, Washington 98272 • (206) 794-7497
Admission: Free. **Hours:** Open during regular hospital hours. Monday–Friday 7am–9pm; Saturday–Sunday 8am–9pm. **To get there:** From I-5, take Highway 2 east to Monroe. The hospital is across from the fairgrounds.

Here's Monte

The House of Poverty

If only half the stories Monte Holm tells are true, his House of Poverty museum in Moses Lake is still astonishing. Holm's tale is a classic rags-to-riches story of poor boy making good, and his homemade museum is a testament to that experience. "You ain't ever seen nothin' like this," Monte tells his visitors. "It's the uniquest museum in the western United States." Monte looks to be somewhere north of 60 and south of 100, and his wardrobe includes a straw hat, tie, and moth-eaten sweater ("I never take 'em off"). He has a stocky build, sharp blue eyes, and a head that's bald as an egg ("The Good Lord made very few perfect heads; the rest he had to put hair on").

"Here," he says, "you better have some candy—it's good for you." Every visitor to the House of Poverty gets a gift, even if it's only candy, and Monte accepts no donations for the extensive tours he gives of his museum. He was a hobo for six years during the Great Depression, and he promised himself then that "if I could ever afford it I'd be good to people." The House of Poverty is his way of paying back those who were kind—and unkind—to him during that time.

Toward the end of his hobo days, "with a dime in my pocket," he decided he'd try his hand at the scrap metal business. Today that business, Moses Lake Iron and Metal, is a huge, bustling, noisy yard that does a brisk trade. Monte presides over it from a tiny office where a massive dog named Sam lies in one corner, workers trundle in and out, friends drop by with gifts of produce, and men in pickups stop to deliver aluminum cans for recycling.

Monte is happy to turn operations over to his assistants when he's called upon to deliver a tour of the museum, which is housed in a large warehouse next to the scrapyard.

Unlike Monte's office, the museum is immaculately clean and extremely well-ordered. The tour begins in a small room that contains some personal mementos—including Monte's daughter's first doll and his father's watch chain. Inside the same glass case is a ratty-looking necktie identified by a handwritten tag as one that Monte wore "every day for 25 years—it looks like it's leather but it's not—too much soup."

Part of Monte's huge and eclectic collection: hundreds of original branding irons, one of which, Monte says, is the first ever used in the Northwest, a "Box" brand dating from the 1860s, used by "an Indian who ran horses between Coeur d'Alene and Spokane." Also on display: a Singer sewing machine "that once belonged to a relative of the James boys"; a whistle from the first steamship on the West Coast; 1930s-vintage quack medico-electrical devices; the whistle ("Big Ole") from the biggest sawmill in the world, the now-defunct Bloedel Donovan mill in Bellingham; a gun that arrived from England on the Mayflower ("It's about my age"); a chamber pot from the Central Pacific Railroad; and an antique dentist's chair ("I do a little dental work to supplement my income, so if anybody has a toothache . . .").

Some of the collection is genuinely collectible—the 1919 Stutz fire engine, for example, one of only six known to exist—while some is strictly sentimental—a nondescript brick, for instance. One freezing night during his hobo days, a kindly sheriff let Monte sleep in the Havre, Montana, jailhouse; when Monte found out years later that the jail was being torn down, he arranged to get one of its bricks. In his career as a junk dealer, Monte has dismantled 23 railroads. The centerpiece of his railroad collection, outside the museum, is a 1915 private rail car, formerly owned by the president of the Northern Pacific and used on separate occasions by Presidents Wilson and Truman. Monte declines to say how much he paid when he bought it in the 1970s, but he

does divulge that Burlington Northern put $80,000 into restoring it just prior to the sale.

The car—84 tons of steel, 90 feet long, and named "The Ruth M" after Monte's wife—has been beautifully restored inside and out. The dining room, for instance, features lace tablecloths, hardwood cupboards, and original china. "I got kicked off so many trains, and I always said I'd buy one someday," Monte says. "Now I use it as my camper."

The House of Poverty, Moses Lake Iron and Metal • PO Box 448, Moses Lake, Washington 98837 • (509) 765-6342
Admission: Free. Hours: Mon–Fri 9am–5pm; other times by appointment. To get there: Exit from I-90 at Moses Lake and drive along Broadway until you see the steam locomotives. The office of Moses Lake Iron and Metal is just behind them.

Beyond Twin Peaks

NORTH BEND
NORTH BEND
Snoqualmie Valley Historical Museum

Hollywood shone its spotlight on this area during the filming of the "Twin Peaks" television show and movie, and
tourists still flock here seeking the cherry pie and "damned
fine cup of coffee" consumed by the show's characters. Just down
the road from the Mar-T Cafe, the restaurant made famous by TV,
the Snoqualmie Valley Historical Museum sits quietly in Gardiner
Weeks Park. The museum, not the restaurant, is where visitors
can get a taste of the area's true history and culture.

This is one of the cleanest and brightest historical museums
we've seen. It's small, but it addresses the history of both the

A rare photograph of women loggers.

Snoqualmie Indian tribe and the European and American pioneers who came to log and farm in the area. Many of the baskets on display were given to area settlers by Chief Jerry Kanim, and the fiddle here was played at many of the area's early dances.

Kids will love "Fuzzy," the preserved, stuffed 2-year-old bear cub by the front door who was shot by mistake a few years back, as well as the fully stocked 1912 country kitchen complete with a baby doll in the high chair waiting for breakfast.

Out back there's a clean, well-stocked farm shed, where everything is clearly identified, from the lovely tall green metal-and-glass Rainbow gas pump to the small but curious-looking industrial egg grader. If the shed is locked, just ask for the key at the desk.

Snoqualmie Valley Historical Museum • 320 North Bend Boulevard, PO Box 179, North Bend, Washington 98045 • (206) 888-3200
Admission: By donation. Hours: Apr–Oct: Sat–Sun 1pm–5pm; also open the first two weekends in Dec. To get there: From I-90 take exit 31; the museum is just north of the outlet mall on North Bend Boulevard.

A Duck-billed Platypus

OLYMPIA
Washington State Capitol Museum

The Washington State Capitol Museum is housed in Lord Mansion, an impressive red-tile–roofed house with 32 rooms and five fireplaces, built in the early 1920s for the family of banker C. J. Lord, who served as Olympia's mayor from 1902 to 1903. The wood-paneled rooms in which Lord held formal dinner parties now house an eclectic collection, including Native American basketry shaped around bottles, a 30-day clock that once hung in the state's legislative chambers, a platypus, and a piece of the moon that NASA gave to the state of Washington.

According to curator Drew Crooks, the moon rock "doesn't glow or anything," but visitors who want to see the small rock may make an appointment to view it.

The museum is dedicated to preserving the history and culture of the state capital—items relating to Washington territorial and state government, as well as artifacts representing the daily life of the Native American tribes of the Puget Sound area. A permanent exhibit of special note is the re-created Native American cedar winterhouse, featuring an audiotape and hands-on exhibits.

Kids will enjoy rocking the cradle, handling the fishing and basket-weaving tools, testing the mortar and pestle, and learning about the salmon-drying process.

Washington State Capitol Museum • 211 W 21st Avenue, Olympia, Washington 98501 • (206) 753-2580
Admission: By donation. **Hours:** Tues–Fri 10am–4pm, Sat–Sun 12pm–4pm. **To get there:** From I-5, take the State Capitol exit and head straight ahead to the capitol campus. At the light on Capitol Way take a left, then take a right on 21st.

Sea Shells and Sea Devils

PORT GAMBLE
Museum of Shells and Marine Life

The town of Port Gamble looks so perfect and cute, you may feel as if you've stepped into a postcard. But it's real. Since the 1850s Port Gamble has been a working mill town, with the oldest continuously operating lumber mill in North America. Still, the New England–style company-owned town has been declared a National Historic Site, and signs on the well-cared-for front lawns tell a bit of history about each house and building.

The Country Store Building houses a real country store and two very different museums. At the back of the building you'll find the entrance to the Port Gamble Historic Museum, which tells the story of the area's lumber industry. Upstairs from the store is the Museum of Shells and Marine Life.

The shell museum is an "exploded biology project" put together by Port Gamble resident Tom Rice over 40 years. While

less than half of Rice's collection of 16,000 shells and several thousand specimens of marine life is on display, you'll still have plenty to see: giant Australian false trumpet snails (at 3 feet across, the largest shells in the world), whale barnacles, whale lice, and every shape, size, and color of shellfish you can imagine. Rice and his museum volunteers organized an impressive display of mother-of-pearl and abalone shells alongside shells sporting natural dots, circles, spirals, and perfectly formed triangle designs.

If there are small children in your party, you may want to steer clear of the sea creature mounted by the window at the end of the second-floor balcony. From a short distance it looks like a shrunken flying monkey. Step closer and you'll learn that in Mexico they call these dried preserved skate carcasses "sea devils." Just when you thought it was safe to go back in the water. . .

Museum of Shell and Marine Life • PO Box 219, Rainier Avenue, Port Gamble, Washington 98364 • (206) 297-2426
Admission: Free. Hours: Memorial Day–Labor Day: every day 10am–4pm. To get there: The museum is on the second floor of the general store in "downtown" Port Gamble on SR 104. The Port Gamble Historic Museum is located in the basement of the general store.

Life in a Log Cabin

PORT ORCHARD
Sidney Museum and Log Cabin Museum

Port Orchard's original name, Sidney, was given to it by the man who laid out the town in 1884. As shipping and logging grew in importance, the town took a more appropriate name, Port Orchard, in 1903.

The Sidney Museum is located on the second floor of a former Masonic hall that also houses an art gallery. It features displays depicting the production of terra-cotta pottery, which was among the town's successful early businesses, and life-size diaromas of the old dry-goods store and the doctor's office. Try to figure out how only one of the 23 original 1909 ballroom chairs from the Governor's Mansion in Olympia ended up here, all alone.

A short but strenuous walk up Sidney Street takes you to the Log Cabin Museum. No problem figuring out how this one got its name—it's a log cabin, built in 1903, and the volunteer on duty made a point of telling us that every log used in its construction was dragged up the hill from the beach by its original occupants.

The Sidney Association decided that any old volunteer group could stock a cabin with historical items and costumed mannequins and call it a museum. So, to make their community different, they created an imaginary mannequin family and a changing family story to go with seasonal "set changes" in the cabin. When we visited, the Orchards' house was decorated for Christmas 1942, and almost everyone was caught up in war-related activities. Lewis and Emelia their children Emily, Charles, and Teddy, and even Grandma Lydia were all busy rolling bandages, counting food ration stamps, or preparing literature about curfews and blackout regulations. Upstairs in the cramped, converted attic, cousin Sadie and her sailor husband, William, were packing a duffel bag so he'd be ready to set out for naval training school back East. Corny as it sounds, the invented family life does help set a period mood and bring the objects in each room alive. You can read the story on a printed flier, but it's more fun to have the docent tell it to you as you walk through the cabin.

Sidney Museum • 202 Sidney Avenue, Port Orchard, Washington 98366 • (206) 876-3693
Admission: Free. Hours: Tues–Sat 11am–4pm, Sun 1pm–5pm. To get there: Sidney Avenue goes sharply uphill from Bay Street in Port Orchard .

Log Cabin Museum • 416 Sidney Avenue, Port Orchard, Washington 98366 • (206) 876-3693
Admission: Free. Hours: Tues 10am–12pm, Sat 11am–4pm, Sun 1pm–4pm; other times by appointment. To get there: Sidney Avenue goes sharply uphill from Bay Street in Port Orchard.

Unearthing a Culture

Chinese Artifact Display, Port Townsend Antique Mall

Chinese laborers came to the Northwest in the mid-1850s to work on building the railroad. When that job ended, many of the laborers and their families settled in places like Port Townsend, finding work in the lumber mills, the canneries, the mines, and local businesses.

A few years ago workers excavating an empty lot in downtown Port Townsend uncovered artifacts from the Chinese community that had been centered there 100 years earlier. Schoolchildren were invited to help sift through the excavated dirt for more, and local history enthusiasts combed old city maps and records for information.

The maps revealed that several businesses had been on the site, including a food store, a laundry, and a brothel. And records disclosed that a fire in the late 1890s probably destroyed the original buildings. The recovered artifacts, now on display in the lower floor of the antique mall built in the same location, provide curious and informative glimpses into life in the Chinese community.

The display includes everyday items such as medicine bottles, marbles, rice bowls, coins, gambling buttons, and bottles. But sifters also found wild boar tusks, opium pipes, a child's toy, and something very mysterious: a .32-caliber bullet in a cone-shaped ink bottle from 1885. There was still ink in the bottle, suggesting to amateur detectives such as ourselves that a century ago, someone found a very good hiding spot.

Port Townsend Antique Mall • 802 Washington Street, Port Townsend, Washington 98368 • (206) 385-2590
Admission: Free, Hours: Mon–Fri 9:30am–5pm, Sat 9:30am–5:30pm, Sun 10am–5pm. **To get there:** Follow Route 20 into town to Water Street. Turn left on Adams Street. Go one block to Washington Street.

A Narrow Escape

PORT TOWNSEND
Jefferson County
Historical Museum

In 1854 the U.S. Customs Service moved its regional office to Port Townsend from Olympia, making the city the official port of entry to Puget Sound. Port Townsend became an important trading and supply center, and later prospered from the timber industry. Today, many of the town's homes and downtown storefronts retain their original or restored Victorian look, and the area has been a National Historical District since 1976.

The Jefferson County Historical Museum fills four floors of the 1892 City Hall building. Visitors enter the museum through what was once the municipal court. Native American baskets and artifacts are on view, along with Victorian furniture and equipment, and items used by the early Chinese residents of the town. The judge's high wooden bench and the witness box are still intact, and the witness box contains two chairs garishly decorated with buffalo horns and bearskins. Witnesses didn't have to testify from these fearsome seats; they were used for portrait sittings by a local photographer in the 1890s and are now are just stored here.

The old fire hall displays military and maritime artifacts and a collection of over 6,000 catalogued historic photographs. Up a flight of stairs, in the old hayloft, you'll find Victorian toys and one of the museum's more unusual holdings: Emillie Rothschild's napkin ring collection, which includes rings made from silver, whalebone, seashells, teak, buffalo horn, porcelain, and human hair, brought to her from all over the world.

The old firemen's quarters at the top of the building house a research and genealogy library, the Bash family's collection of seashells, coral, and stuffed birds, and part of Mrs. McIlroy's button collection.

Whenever 10-year-old Port Townsend resident John Steurer visits the museum, as he did when we were there, he rushes past the furry chairs and the napkin rings and heads straight downstairs to the old jail cells. He says it's his favorite part, even though "just thinking about having to be in one of these cold, leaky things" scares him. John asked research librarian Betty Pfouts to tell him the story of Howard Garner, who was being held in the solitary confinement cell back in 1926. Somehow Garner escaped by squeezing his body through the slim slot in the cell door, the one only big enough to pass a tray of food through. Pfouts said that another prisoner had tried the same escape route a few years earlier, but got his head stuck in the slot and was found there dead in the morning.

Jefferson County Historical Museum • 210 Madison Street, Port Townsend, Washington 98368 • (206) 385-1003

Admission: By donation. **Hours:** Mon–Sat 11am–4pm, Sun 1pm–4pm. **To get there:** Go north through downtown Port Townsend on Water Street and turn left at Madison Street. The museum is in the historic City Hall building.

The Disappearing Guns and the Buried Locomotive

PORT TOWNSEND
Puget Sound Coast Artillery Museum

Fort Casey (on Whidbey Island), Fort Flagler (on Marrowstone Island), and Fort Worden, here in Port Townsend, were all built at the turn of the century as seacoast artillery defense stations protecting the harbors and waterways of Puget Sound. Deactivated as a military post in 1953, Fort Worden, which overlooks the Strait of Juan de Fuca and Admiralty Inlet, is now a 446-acre state park with restored Victorian officers' houses, barracks, artillery bunkers, and a conference center. Its picturesque setting provided the romantic backdrop for the movie *An Officer and a Gentleman*, and the fort's original dirigible hangar (now the Mc-Curdy Pavilion performance hall) was used to shoot scenes for the movie. Park visitors can rent an officers'-row house overnight, or

Unearthing a steam locomotive that was buried in the sand for 60 years.

spend a day walking on the beach, touring the restored Commanding Officer's Quarters, and paying a visit to the Puget Sound Coast Artillery Museum.

If, like us, you don't have much military or artillery history under your belt, ask museum director Keith Hogan to run the short video. It features archival footage of Fort Worden activities, including shots of the huge "disappearing guns" that were kept at the ready from 1910 until 1943. Working models (they disappear but don't shoot) of those guns are on display at the museum. Hogan says that many veterans stop by the museum, but just about anyone would be interested in the military uniform collection dating back to the turn of the century, and in the story behind the resurrection of a steam locomotive that was buried at the fort for more than 60 years.

The locomotive, which will be displayed as soon as the museum can figure out how to keep people from climbing on it, was used between 1890 and 1910 in the construction of both Fort Flagler and Fort Worden. Like much of the other equipment used in the fortification efforts of the time, the engine was supposed to be destroyed after it served its usefulness. In 1911 Colonel Garland Whistler turned down a $30 offer for the scrap metal in the

locomotive. Instead, for unknown reasons, he gave the order to have it buried in the sand. A storage shed was later built over the site and people forgot about it until 1973, when the shed was demolished and someone noticed a piece of rusty metal sticking out of the ground.

Puget Sound Coast Artillery Museum • **200 Battery Way, Fort Worden State Park, Port Townsend, Washington 98368** • **(206) 385-0373**
Admission: By donation. **Hours:** Call for hours. **To get there:** Follow Cherry Street from downtown Port Townsend to Fort Worden State Park.

Revisit the West

PULLMAN
Three Forks Pioneer Museum

W hen Stella Rossebo came to this 420-acre farm 55 years ago, there was nothing on the land but a tiny log cabin dating from 1885. Visit the Three Forks Pioneer Museum today and you will not believe that statement. Piece by piece, building by building, wooden plank by wooden plank, over the past 40 years Stella and her son Roger have re-created a full-size, late 19th-century Western town on their farmland.

They built it all by themselves, and over time they've collected and been given the thousands of antique items that fill the doctor's office (with a Marilyn Monroe lookalike on the operating table), the millinery store, the barbershop, the pharmacy, the general store, the dentist's office, the tin-ceilinged saloon, the butcher shop, the creamery, the hardware store, the blacksmith shop, and, of course, the jail. Stella will be happy to tell you elaborate stories about the daily goings-on of the owners and workers in each store.

There's also a peek-a-boo park for kids, with a rock garden filled with leprechaun statues, dollhouses, plastic chickens, and a tiny pet cemetery. Two small houses in the children's corner are filled floor-to-ceiling with toys—one with dolls, the other with 100 teddy bears and what Stella terms "boy toys." And Stella has planted flowers everywhere.

Three Forks Pioneer Museum • Rt 1 Box 290, Albion Road, Pullman, Washington 99163 • (509) 332-3889
Admission: $2 for adults, discounts for children. **Hours:** May–Oct: Mon–Sat, by appointment only. **To get there:** From Pullman, drive north on Highway 27; turn left on Albion Road and go 2 miles. Turn right on Anderson Road. Go 2.8 miles to Rossebo's Farm and Museum, which will be on the right-hand side of the road. Look for signs.

As Old as the Woods

PULLMAN: WASHINGTON STATE UNIVERSITY
The Lyle and Lela Jacklin Petrified Wood Collection

To the untrained eye, a piece of unpolished petrified wood from an ancient forest looks just like any old branch or stump in the woods, but try to pick up a piece. It may look like a piece of wood, but it feels like heavy rock. Sliced and polished, the wood is also beautiful, and some kinds, such as "picture jasper," look as if someone has painted a delicate cityscape on them.

Before Lyle and Lela Jacklin donated their petrified wood collection to the university, the 1,700 specimens were scattered all over their house. The Jacklins collected much of the wood themselves on trips throughout the West, but the story goes that Lyle also had a forest "connection," a hermit living in the woods who cut fossilized wood for him.

A few display cases with samples of petrified wood and minerals are visible in the front hall of the Physical Sciences Building, but the bulk of the collection is in Room 124. Though the cases here are jam-packed, they're not as stuffed as they used to be because many duplicate samples were recently removed. "You literally couldn't see the forest for the trees," said our tour guide, without even a hint of a smile.

Once you've had your fill of petrified wood, agates, and colorful geodes, step behind a curtain where glow-in-the-dark rocks reveal wild neon colors when exposed to ultraviolet light.

The Lyle and Lela Jacklin Petrified Wood Collection • Physical Sciences Building, Room 124 • (509) 335-3009

Herbal Delights

PULLMAN: WASHINGTON STATE UNIVERSITY
The Marion Ownby Herbarium

In this herbarium, or plant museum, curator Joy Mastrogiuseppe explains that plants get pressed on paper "because you can't stuff a plant like an animal." The university's collection, started in the late 1800s, focuses on Northwest plants, although there are specimens here of plants from around the world.

Not many casual visitors browse through the 300,000 specimens stored in the tall, rolling file cabinets, but members of the general public often come by with something they want identified. One curious local brought in a packet containing chicken gizzards and wanted help identifying the seeds found inside them.

We thought this was a good opportunity to ask someone who spends their days around plants if talking to them is really a good idea. "Doesn't hurt," Mastrogiuseppe offered, "but actually it's more soothing for the people who do the talking."

The Marion Ownby Herbarium • Heald Hall, Room G9 • (509) 335-3250

Fleas and Flies

PULLMAN: WASHINGTON STATE UNIVERSITY
Maurice James Entomological Collection

Curator Richard Zak has eaten his share of insects, but he assured us that he doesn't "bring them for lunch every day." Zak, who is in charge of the university's century-old insect collection, reports that at last count there were more than a million butterflies, fleas, flies, beetles, and creepy-crawly specimens, all pinned, dried, and resting comfortably in drawers. Included among the holdings are a rare California butterfly that became extinct in the 1940s and a tankful of definitely alive giant Madagascar cockroaches.

The place smells faintly of camphor, which Zak says is because until recently mothballs were stored among the insects to keep uninvited bugs from feasting on the collection. Now every specimen that arrives goes first into the freezer for a day or so; that eliminates the need for mothballs.

While activities are mostly research-oriented, the department does answer questions from the public. Often, Zak says, people call up to describe a bug that's just bitten them, wanting advice on whether (or how much) they should worry. Other times, would-be entomologists put an insect in an envelope and send it in for identification.

This is the type of place that kids love, and department representatives will often put together a drawerful of notable insects for scheduled groups. More than likely, the sampling will include a giant 4-inch cockroach, several colorful beetles and butterflies, a 7-inch grasshopper, and flies no bigger than the head of a pin.

Maurice James Entomological Collection • Food Science Building, Room 157 • (509) 335-5504

Ancient Jewels

PULLMAN: WASHINGTON STATE
UNIVERSITY
The Museum of
Anthropology

The university's anthropology museum features exhibits that document the record of human evolution, Eskimo cultural ecology, the settlement of the Pacific Northwest, and the transformation of Native American West Coast basketry from utility to commodity. Although curator Alice Gronski was hesitant to promote it, the museum also has one showcase devoted to the elusive sasquatch.

The sasquatch exhibit includes a cast of footprints and hand-prints, a blow-up of a frame from a filmed sighting, and a map marking sasquatch sightings throughout Washington and Idaho.

The Northwest isn't the only part of the world where sasquatch-type creatures hang out. The museum has a cast made from a giant jaw found in Guangxi, China, in 1957, along with a reconstruction of the huge skull in which the jaw would fit.

The Museum of Anthropology • College Hall • (509) 335-3441

NOTE: Washington State University in Pullman has more than a dozen museums and special collections open to the public. We were there for two days and still couldn't see everything. Among those we missed were the Conner Museum in Science Hall, which boasts the largest public collection of preserved birds and animals in the Pacific Northwest; the Historic Textiles and Costume Collection in White Hall; and the Veterinary Anatomy Museum, in Wegner Hall, which has several hundred specimens but may be too grisly for some children.

To request a brochure listing the museums and collections on campus call the Special Collections office at (509) 335-6272.

Museums and Collections, Washington State University • Pullman, Washington 99164
Admission: Free. Hours: Mon– Fri 8am–5pm during the school year; some collections have limited weekend hours. Outside the school year it's best to call ahead for an appointment. To get there: The Washington State University campus is hard to miss in Pullman. Follow the signs. Once on campus, be sure to stop and get a visitor's parking pass and map of the campus.

Fungimania

The Mycological Herbarium

Another working collection, where mycologists come to study fungi. But stop by and they'll be glad to show you some unusual specimens they keep handy just for visitors. These aren't your average backyard mushrooms—one resembles an enlarged human brain, and others are dark and evil-looking.

Curator Jack Rogers notes that the department gets more callers than visitors, and although it's been about 20 years since callers wanted help identifying psychedelic mushrooms, the Walla Walla prison warden did ring up recently. The warden was worried because prisoners were picking mushrooms growing in the exercise yard. Rogers's advice: Pick them before the prisoners do.

And then there's the "biggest mushroom" debate. A few years ago, both Michigan and Washington state claimed to have the largest living fungus. Rogers is disgruntled with this controversy and insists that Washington has the biggest mushroom—located near the base of Mount Adams. He believes, however, that he knows of an even bigger organism in Montana. Stop by, he says, and *maybe* he'll tell you where it is.

The Mycological Herbarium • Johnson Hall, Room 339 • (509) 335-9541

The Joy of Dirt

Smith Soil Monolith Collection

Room 114 in Johnson Hall is the school's soil museum. Here we were gently reminded that soil "is held in higher esteem than everyday dirt." If you find the museum locked, don't fret; just stand outside the door, hold the light switch on, and look through the window to see almost 100 soil "profiles" gathered mostly by Henry Smith, who is remembered as a "scientist who was also an artist." Smith apparently mastered the skill needed to make what are essentially soil "mummies." He'd dig a big pit and carefully extract and wrap intact soil samples up to 8 feet long. Once unwrapped in the laboratory and mounted on the long boards displayed here, soil mummies offer clues to how the land has been changed by volcanic eruptions, earthquakes, and, of course, the sands of time.

Smith Soil Monolith Collection • Johnson Hall, Room 114 • (509) 335-1859

Dig Your Own Fossils

REPUBLIC
Stonerose Interpretive Center and Fossil Site

More varieties of plant fossils have been found at the Stonerose Fossil Site, in the northeastern Washington town of Republic, than at any other paleontological dig in the world—including 210 types of leaves and 35 species of roses.

One of these, the oldest known ancestor of the rose family, provides the site's name.

The fossils at Stonerose are from the Eocene epoch, 47 million to 50 million years ago, some 10 million years after the last of the dinosaurs disappeared. The Cascade range was not yet high enough to affect the weather of eastern Washington, so it was probably wetter and warmer there than it is now. Many broad-leaved trees now native to the Southeast thrived in the area, along with plants now found only in the Far East and varieties that are completely extinct. Republic was once at the bottom of a large lake; over time sediment built up, much of it powdery volcanic ash, and the layers trapped millions of leaves and insects. As the lake dried out, the sediment formed a fine-grained stone called tuff that easily splits apart.

The site has been under study by a group headed by scientists from the University of Washington's Burke Museum and the U.S. Geological Survey since 1977—but it's been open to the public since 1986. A small interpretive center, in a house off the main street in town, has displays of fossils and descriptive text. (Curator Lisa Barksdale, an excellent resource person, is also usually on hand.) Bring your own hammer and chisel, or, for a nominal fee, you can rent fossil hammers at the center, then walk up and dig at the site itself. You're virtually assured of finding fossils—

Stonerose has plenty for everyone. Visitors are allowed to take home up to three fossils a day, although Stonerose keeps close tabs on what's found and reserves the right to keep any that might help its ongoing study. Jeans and sturdy shoes are advised.

Stonerose Interpretive Center • 15 N Kean Street, PO Box 987, Republic, Washington 98166 • (509) 775-2295
Admission: Free. Tool rental is $2.50 per day. **Hours:** May 1–Oct 31, Tues–Sat 10am–5pm. Also, June 1–Sept 30, Sun 10am–5pm. **To get there:** Republic is situated at the intersection of highways 20 and 21 in Ferry County. Follow the signs to the Center.

Atomic Marbles

RICHLAND
Hanford Science Center

In early December 1942 a team of scientists led by Enrico Fermi detonated the world's first controlled nuclear chain reaction. A year later 640 acres of desert near Hanford, Washington—remote, but with railroad access and abundant water and electricity—was chosen as the site for the Manhattan Project, the code name for the U.S. effort to build a nuclear weapon. The next spring, 1,200 residents were evacuated from the communities of Richland, Hanford, and White Bluffs. In their place came construction workers—51,000 of them at the peak of activity—knowing only that they were building something very hush-hush. The work went quickly; a little over two years after construction began, the world's first three plutonium production plants were providing material for the world's first nuclear explosion, in New Mexico.

By 1964 Hanford—which covered 560 square miles, nearly half the size of Rhode Island—had nine plutonium plants and facilities for fuel production, chemical processing, waste management, and research. The focus changed during the 1960s and '70s, as attitudes about atomic power shifted. The reactors gradually shut down and the emphasis shifted from military operations to being an energy-related, semiprivate enterprise. The last production reactor went on "cold standby" in 1988, leaving active only Handford's Fast Flux Test Facility. Some 13,000 people are now involved in cleaning up the site—more than twice the number needed to run it at its peak.

The Hanford Science Center, in the Federal Building in downtown Richland, combines historical photos, artifacts, and hands-on science displays to tell the story of Hanford. No matter what your feelings might be on nuclear energy in general or Hanford in particular, it's a remarkable story.

The first display in the museum is a series of photos depicting small-town desert life before the Army Corps of Engineers arrived in 1943. This segues into photos of the site under construction, and a display of vintage signs ("No Accident Week July

3–10") found during the cleanup process. A research project is currently under way, and eventually thousands of other photographs taken over the years will be catalogued and exhibited. Other displays demonstrate cleanup methods now being tested.

A child-friendly "manipulator" simulates equipment used to handle radioactive material; by moving handles around, you can wield "robot hands" to pick up blocks on the other side of a glass window. A touch-screen computer display determines your own personal radiation dose, based on national averages and the answers to such questions as How far from a nuclear facility do you live? And a gum dispenser will sell you, for a dime, a marble that has been exposed to a Cobalt 60 source. The radiation has turned the marble from clear to greenish-brown. Although a sign on the dispenser assures visitors that the marbles are not radioactive, a further warning is posted: "THIS IS NOT CANDY."

Hanford Science Center • 825 Jadwin Avenue, Richland, Washington 99352 • (509) 376-6374
Admission: Free. **Hours:** Mon–Fri 8am–5pm, Sat 9am–5pm. **To get there:** From Highway 82 take the George Washington Way exit to Richland. Turn left on Lee Boulevard and right on Jadwin Avenue. The Hanford Science Center is between the post office and the Federal Building, which is the tallest building in Richland.

Remember the Battle

ROSALIA
Rosalia Museum

Mayor Warren Roellich of Rosalia says his town's museum is always open during Battle Days—the first weekend in June—which he says is also the best time to visit. Battle Days commemorates the infamous 1858 battle between the U.S. Army, led by Lt. Col. Edward J. Steptoe, and members of several of the area's Native American tribes. Steptoe's troops were soundly defeated, and Mayor Roellich says he believes Rosalia is today "the only town that celebrates a battle where the Indians won." The Steptoe Memorial on Seventh Street, and a sign at the edge of town that reminds drivers to "Remember the Battle," also commemorate the event.

If you can't make it to Battle Days, you may find Rosalia a little sleepy and the museum locked up tight. When we stopped in town on a 100-degree day, the town clerk was on vacation and the library was closed, so it seemed that we'd have to miss the Rosalia Museum, housed in City Hall. We stopped for ice cream at the grocery store, and the checkers suggested we call the mayor to see if someone could open the museum for us. Mayor Roellich put down the sandwich he was having for lunch, jumped in his truck, and drove the block and a half from his house to open the museum for us.

The mayor did more than just open up the museum. Admitting that he hadn't been inside in quite a while, he joined us on a tour of the holdings. Along with memorabilia from area residents, the museum displays a piece of a meteor found south of Rosalia, a wishing well, a metal bathtub, and the town's original jail cell. Roellich remembers the last time it was used, back in 1945, and says the town stopped using it because it was too easy for prisoners to escape. Now cardboard cutouts of wine-cooler ad men sit inside it. Stored above the cell is a casket once used during funeral services at one of the local churches.

Rosalia Museum • W 106 5th Street, PO Box 277, Rosalia, Washington 99170 • (509) 523-5991
Admission: Free. Hours Tues–Fri 8am–5pm; Sat 10am–1pm. To get there: On Business Route 195 in Rosalia, watch for a small wooden sign that says "Museum" at 5th Street. The museum is located in the same building as the library and City Hall, and is open whenever the library is open, or when someone is at City Hall.

Mrs. Meek's Black Leggins

Roslyn Museum

At the turn of the century, the coal fields around Roslyn were among the most extensive on the West Coast, drawing workers from a long list of ethnic groups. Oil and hydro-electric power eventually replaced the need for Roslyn's coal, and by the mid-1960s all the local coal mines were shut down. But the town of Roslyn lives on and its mining history is preserved in the Roslyn Museum, which features samples of coal from the area mines, mining equipment, and beer taps from some of the 23 saloons the boomtown once supported.

Mary Andler is the Roslyn Museum curator, and you'll want to be sure that's she's on duty when you visit, because she's the one who knows the stories that go along with the items in the museum. As with many small-town historical museums, everything here once belonged to someone who lived in town. But unlike other museums, where the curator picks and chooses among offerings, when a townsperson comes by and says, "Mary, would you like to have this for the museum?" Andler says she doesn't turn anything down. You can tell.

There's no kitchen sink here, but the museum does have the town's first electric refrigerator. It arrived in 1923 and belonged to Dr. Low, the dentist. Up front there's an assortment of alarm clocks, cameras, pens from area businesses, family albums, and an old button accordion "played for many, many dances in town." Black "leggins used by Mrs. Meek in the early days" are also on display, along with blueprints of the local mine where 45 men were killed in an 1892 explosion, a 5-foot-long YMCA wooden dumbbell, and a homemade bear trap.

Framed and hung on the back wall is a letter from Bing Crosby confirming that his family lived in Roslyn for a few years, that his dad worked at the company store, and that his brother Everett was born there. On the grass outside the museum you'll see coal cars, an outhouse (kept locked—it's just for show), and the old Kerstetter log cabin, built in the nearby town of Liberty in 1932. A Boy Scout troop took the cabin apart and rebuilt it on-site.

Andler says it used to take a year for the museum to get 3,000 visitors, but since the popular television show "Northern Exposure" has been filmed here, the museum has tallied more than 10,000 signatures in the guestbook. Money from the increased admissions will be used to rewire the building, put new "old-time" siding on, and perhaps build an extension, but the "town attic" quality of the displays will stay the same.

Roslyn Museum • 28 Pennsylvania Avenue, Roslyn, Washington 98941 • (509) 649-2776
Admission: By donation. **Hours:** Every day, 1pm–5pm. **To get there:** From Eastbound I-90 take exit 80. The museum is in the center of town, right next to the Roslyn Cafe (made famous by "Northern Exposure").

A Triceratops Horn and Other Ancient Clues

SEATTLE
Geology Collection, Burke Museum

The Burke Museum at the University of Washington, founded in 1885, is the only major natural-history museum in the Northwest. It is also a world-class museum of anthropology, with an emphasis on the people of the Pacific Rim and Washington State. It has fascinating permanent and changing exhibits, but—as is true with most museums—only a tiny fraction of the Burke's 5 million objects can be on display at one time.

Special tours of some of the collections not on public display can sometimes be arranged. But where to start? With the brilliant

assembly of masks, sculpture, canoes, weapons, and other artifacts from all along the Pacific Rim? The 4,000 Native American baskets? The outdoor exhibit of totem poles? The computer display that gives access to 13,000 pieces in the Pacific Northwest collection? Or the 10,000 bird skeletons and 21,500 bird skins that compose just a part of the ornithology collection? The 38,000 butterflies? The 64,000 spiders? The samples of one of the world's largest fleas, the fearsome-looking *Dolichopsyllus stylosus*, found in the Northwest on mountain beavers?

Okay, let's examine just one section. How about geology? This division maintains the museum's paleontology and mineral collections. On permanent display in the museum's main halls are a number of dinosaur skeletons (the only ones on view in the Northwest), a touchable track cast of an allosaurus, a crocodile-like skeleton from Japan, fossilized wood, and a box with phosphorescent rocks that can be seen when you turn on the UV light. A couple of hundred of these geology specimens are on display at any given time, and some are changed every month or so.

In the Burke's windowless basement, the Geology Division's affable collections manager, Ron Eng, oversees the rest of his grouping: a kingdom that includes some five million invertebrate, vertebrate, and plant fossils, along with modern mollusks (clams and snails). Much of the material here is valuable for research purposes, Eng says, but it is not necessarily museum-quality or of burning interest to the public. It's a low-key operation, with a small staff and a loyal core of regular volunteers who help out with the staggering amounts of data. (Most of this data is not on computer, but it is slowly being transferred to disk.)

You want vertebrate fossils? The Burke has 'em—over 40,000 catalogued specimens, enough to rank 22nd out of 109 recognized collections in the United States.

Another room holds the paleobotany collection. A highlight here is the Tuggle collection of fossilized picture woods—small slabs of highly polished fossilized wood. It's easy to discern trees, woods, beaches, and other scenes in their beautiful, bright colors and striations; it's a little like looking at clouds and recognizing unlikely shapes. Another important part of this collection is the grouping of Eocene fossilized plants found in Republic, Washington, by Burke paleobotanist Wesley Wehr (see the entry on the Stonerose Fossil Site).

NOTE: Although some of the Burke's collections are strictly for research and are not open to the public, interested individuals or groups can sometimes obtain special permission to see certain holdings. As is true with the other research collections mentioned in this book, your consideration and thoughtfulness will go a long way toward gaining you admission.

Thomas Burke Memorial Washington State Museum • University of Washington DB-10, Seattle, Washington 98195 • (206) 543-5590
Admission: $3 for adults, discounts for students and senior citizens. Hours: Every day, 10am–5pm, Geology Division by appointment only. To get there: The Burke is located just inside the university's north entrance on 45th Street NE. Ask at the gate for directions to the proper parking area.

Wo-He-Lo

Camp Fire Boys and Girls
Museum

I n 1910 a prominent Maine educator, Dr. Luther H. Gulick, along with his wife, Charlotte, and their friend William Langdon, founded the organization called Camp Fire Girls to "promote the spiritual ideals of home and stimulate healthy, character-building habits." Dr. Gulick had helped organize the Boy Scouts of America, and he wanted to do something similar for his daughters.

Over the years millions of children have learned the principles summarized in the slogan Wo-He-Lo (work, health, love) coined by Mrs. Gulick. Many of Camp Fire's time-honored activities are still part of the curriculum: summer camp, educational programs during the school year, and selling Camp Fire Mints as a fund-raising activity. Other aspects of Camp Fire have changed: its programs went co-ed in the 1970s, and in 1989 its name was officially changed to Camp Fire Boys and Girls.

The only museum anywhere devoted to Camp Fire memorabilia is in a basement room of the Seattle-area council headquarters. (Other regional councils, including Camp Fire national headquarters in Kansas City, have display cases of material, but only Seattle has made a serious effort to catalogue and permanently display its collection.) The volunteer staff are former Camp Fire members, and the material on display has likewise been donated by former members of the organization. Many donations come from "The Black Bloomers," old-timers who are so named because voluminous drawers were once part of their uniform. (Some Camp Fire Girls of that era were known to hide food in their bloomers at mealtimes for late-night snacks.)

Ceremonial Camp Fire dresses are on display, including a Bluebird outfit from 1913 with felt feathers on its wings, and a beautiful 1930s Plains Indian–style gown, adorned with beads and

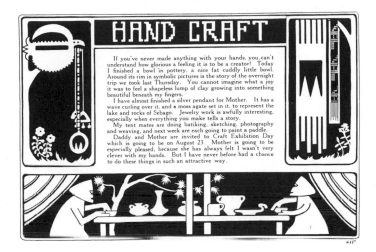

emblems. Also on view: vintage cookbooks, manuals on ceremonial dress, examples of typical crafts such as block printing and woodcraft, and some great 1915-vintage postcards with captions like "Firmly standing girl believes in good posture" and "Taming a chipmunk is nature lore at first hand" (the latter shows a Camp Fire Girl holding a water glass with a chipmunk balanced on its rim!).

There's also a shrine to one of Camp Fire's most beloved products: Until the late 1940s or early 1950s, Camp Fire Girls sold doughnuts and daffodils as fund-raisers. But there were persistent problems with keeping these items fresh, so eventually they switched to selling mints. On the floor in a corner of the museum is a pile of Camp Fire Girl Mint boxes of various vintages. (Volunteer Laurie Scott says, "They're always in a big mess because the kids like to play with them.") And, yes, you can buy a box of mints upstairs.

Camp Fire Boys and Girls Museum • 8511 15th Avenue NE, Seattle, Washington 98115 • (206) 461-8550
Admission: Free. **Hours:** By appointment only. **To get there:** The council headquarters are on the northwest corner of NE 85th Street and 15th Avenue NE in the Maple Leaf neighborhood.

A Tradition of Boats

Center for Wooden Boats/
Northwest Seaport

Boat liveries were common sights on the shores of cities along Puget Sound in the 1920s and 1930s. Renting a sailboat for a day's voyage or taking a rowboat out for a couple of hours of fishing was a typical (and inexpensive) pastime during the Great Depression. The Center for Wooden Boats, at the south end of Lake Union, re-creates the atmosphere of such a facility. A combination museum and workshop, it has a single but broad-based purpose: to preserve and teach all of the arts and sciences, the romance and history, connected with wooden boats. For the center's founder and guiding light, Dick Wagner, maritime history is the key to understanding the Northwest; building or repairing a wooden boat, meanwhile, requires such diverse skills as mathematics, carpentry, physics, chemistry, art, and metalworking.

The center is located on a sliver of lakeshore set off from the busy semi-industrial streets around it by a line of trees and a wooden pavilion. An enclosed yard sports a flagpole with a replica of the "Don't Tread on Me" Navy Jack adopted by the Continental (revolutionary) Navy in 1775. A number of antique wooden canoes from groups as diverse as the Nootka, Salish, and Makah tribes of the Northwest Coast and the Cuna tribe from the Caribbean coast of Panama surround the pavilion. One of the most interesting of these is a small Samoan fishing boat, made of breadfruit wood and sewn together with coconut fiber.

Beyond the pavilion are the center's handsome wooden buildings. One is a repair shop, filled with the fragrance of sawn wood and crowded with friendly volunteers working on boats in various stages of completion. Another building houses meeting rooms, classrooms, offices, and a reference library; it's decorated with handsome student-built kayaks and a racing shell built by the famed Seattle boatbuilder George Pocock. Outside, the center's docks are crowded with its boat collection—the largest in the Northwest. Sixty to 75 boats are on display at any given time, with another 50 or so in storage or in the process of repair. They run the gamut from pleasure boat to workboat: peapods, dories, sharpies, catboats, Hampton boats, Lake Oswego boats, Whitehall boats, Poulsbo boats, canoes, kayaks, skiffs, Stars.

The center holds classes and workshops on a variety of maritime subjects: boatbuilding, knot-tying, maritime history, metalcasting, foundry work, woodworking. It also sponsors workshops for kids and classes for the disabled. "In most museums the things on display just sit there," Wagner says. "Here, maritime history is alive in the teaching of techniques. It's no big secret that the brain will click on when the hands start moving."

In keeping with the center's philosophy of hands-on learning, nearly all of the boats, even historic ones, are available for use. Visitors with basic boating experience can rent the smaller sailboats, paddleboats, or rowboats; more complex sailboats are skippered by experienced sailors who volunteer to take visitors out.

Next door to the Center for Wooden Boats is Northwest Seaport, another nonprofit organization that shelters the historic

The 1897 *Wawona* is one of the largest three-masted schooners ever built in the Northwest.

schooner *Wawona*. The *Wawona*—at 165 feet, one of the largest three-masted schooners ever built in the Northwest—dates from 1897, and is the only survivor of the area's once-thriving commercial sailing fleet. The first ship to be listed on the National Register of Historic Sites, it is still being restored but is open for tours. When additional moorage becomes available, two other boats on the Historic Landmark list—the 129-foot sail/steam light-ship *Relief*, built in 1904, and the 1889 tugboat *Arthur Foss*, 112.5 feet in length—will be moved to the site as well.

Center for Wooden Boats • 1010 Valley Street, Seattle, Washington 98109 • (206) 382-2628
Admission: Rowing/paddling craft $8 to $14 per hour; sailing craft $10 to $25 per hour; tours "and advice" are free. **Hours:** June–Labor Day: every day 11am–7pm; Sept–June: Wed–Mon 12pm–6pm. **To get there:** From I-5, take the Mercer Street exit to Fairview Avenue, then turn into the center's parking lot right after Burger King. Watch for the 30-foot sailboat in the parking lot.

Northwest Seaport • 1002 Valley Street, Seattle, Washington 98109 • (206) 447-9800
Admission: $1 for adults, discounts for children. **Hours:** 10am–5pm; longer in summer, so call ahead for changes. **To get there:** See Center for Wooden Boats, above.

A Piece of the Bounty

SEATTLE
Coast Guard Museum

The New England–style white clapboard building just inside the gate at Seattle's Pier 36, the U.S. Coast Guard facility, was due to be torn down in the mid-1970s. Fortunately for maritime history buffs, it was instead turned into a museum devoted to the Coast Guard—one of only two in the nation, the other being in New London, Connecticut. The museum opened in 1976 and is staffed by volunteers, mostly retired Coasties, who give tours and explain some of the more obscure items.

The museum is eclectic, but it's all nautical. It includes over 20 scale ship models, an 1850s-vintage lighthouse clock, working lights from lighthouses (including the New Dungeness light, in service from 1857 to 1976), and such tools as flare guns and flare pots. There's a Civil War–era line-throwing gun, vintage flags, and examples of the heavy crockery used on Coast Guard ships.

On one wall is a small piece of the fabric from the Curtiss NC-4 plane that made the first trip across the Atlantic, in 1919, with Coast Guard men among its crew. Another small piece of history is a fragment of original timber from "Old Ironsides," the USS *Constitution*—arguably the most famous ship in American history, now restored and permanently moored in Boston Harbor.

Some items are not related directly to the Coast Guard. One example is a heart-wrenching exhibit about explorer Robert Scott's ill-fated journey to the South Pole in 1912. Scott and his party reached the Pole only to discover that Roald Amundsen's group had preceded them by weeks. On the return trip, Scott's party ran into bad weather and perished. A few items in a food cache that Scott never reached are on display, accompanied by explanatory photos and text, including a colorful tin of Rountree's Cocoa and a box of wooden matches.

The most unusual item in the museum is a piece of the rudder from HMS *Bounty*. In 1943 a troop transport in the South Pacific commanded by Admiral Byrd was hunting locations for airstrips. The ship put in at Pitcairn Island, where the *Bounty* had been scuttled by its mutinous crew in 1789. The locals, among them descendants of the *Bounty*'s British crew, asked divers on board the troop transport to do some routine salvage work for them. In the process, the divers also recovered what turned out to be the *Bounty*'s rudder. A small fragment of this treasure ended up in the care of the troop transport's cook, who later donated it to the museum. Attached to the tiny piece of wood is a handwritten note from Admiral Byrd authenticating it.

The iceship *Bear* inspires reverence in every Coastie. Built in 1875 for sealing, she sailed on two of Admiral Byrd's expeditions to Antarctica. The ship sank off Nova Scotia in 1963.

The museum has a reference library with thousands of nautical books and a number of videotapes, including footage of actual rescues, and some vintage movies showing Hollywood's version of life on the seas, guaranteed to give any Coastie the giggles. The library cannot loan material, but it is open for use inhouse, and any of its 15,000 photographs can be copied for a fee. There is also a small selection of books, cacheted envelopes, patches, and hats for sale.

Across the driveway, on the fourth floor of the main building at Pier 36, is the Coast Guard's Vessel Traffic Control (VTC) Center. This is Puget Sound's equivalent to air traffic control; it monitors the movements of over 250,000 vessels annually from Cape Flattery to Olympia. All large vessels must comply with the VTC Center's operators; pleasure boats and small commercial craft are not required to report, but are picked up on the radar nonetheless. There is a short slide show, and the 11 directional radar scopes used to monitor ships are visible through the window. A representative is also on hand to answer questions. Open 8am to 4pm daily.

When the two Polar-class icebreakers and the two high-endurance cutters moored at Pier 36 are not in service, the public may visit them. Call for weekend hours.

Coast Guard Museum • Pier 36, 1519 Alaskan Way S, Seattle, Washington 98134 • (206) 286-9608
Admission: Free. Hours: Mon, Wed, Fri 9am–5pm. To get there: The museum is inside the gate of Pier 36, 1 mile south of the Colman Dock ferry terminal.

Petroleana Paradise

General Petroleum Museum

Early car owners hauled gasoline home from the general store or livery stable in 5-gallon cans and poured it into their gas tanks by themselves. A midwesterner named Samuel Bowser invented the gas pump in the 1880s, but it wasn't until 1907 that the world's first gas station appeared—right here in the Northwest, at First and Holgate on Seattle's waterfront.

Appropriately enough, Seattle is also the home of the General Petroleum Museum. This massive collection of "petroleana"—anything and everything relating to the sale of gasoline—belongs to a retired Mobil Oil employee named Jeff Pedersen. It's housed in the second-story loft of a brick building on Capitol Hill, and is easily recognized by the flying-horse neon sign in the window.

Pedersen's pump collection illustrates the entire history of gasoline sales. He has examples of the earliest ones (called "blind pumps" because they dispensed a generic gasoline) as well as the more sophisticated pumps that came later (such as the clock-face pump and the all-glass "showcase" pump, eventually discontinued because people kept driving into it). These lavishly decorated models were created as advertising gimmicks when the federal government forced the Rockefeller family to give up its oil monopoly and a rush of competing companies jockeyed for customers.

The General Petroleum Museum has hundreds of other items as well, all meticulously catalogued and displayed. There are elaborate service-station signs, highly decorative antique oil cans, and vintage "giveaways" such as plates, toys, and candles, all embossed with company names and logos. There's a mechanical toy pony named Peggy—another of those ubiquitous flying horses. There's even a full-scale replica of an art deco–era service station designed to look like a Roman temple, built right into the middle of the museum.

Pedersen, a husky and garrulous man with a penchant for suspenders emblazoned with red horses, lives with his wife in the loft that houses his collection. They regularly travel around the country, buying petroleana to swap with the surprisingly large numbers

of collectors across America who are crazy about it. Since the museum's space includes an industrial-size kitchen, the Pedersens also rent it out for catered events such as wedding receptions or club meetings.

General Petroleum Museum • 1526 Bellevue Avenue E, Seattle, Washington 98101 • (206) 323-4789
Admission: Free. Hours: By appointment only. To get there: The museum is on the second floor of a brick building on the corner of Bellevue Avenue E and Pine Street on Capitol Hill. The entrance is in the back.

Evel's Helmet and Ali's Shorts

The Royal Brougham Collection, Kingdome Sports Museum

The Kingdome is Seattle's way of reconciling a love of sports with inclement weather. Since 1976 "the Dome" has hosted professional sports games as well as such diverse events as rock concerts, Alcoholics Anonymous conventions, trade shows, and monster truck rallies (which use rented dirt).

Tucked away in a corner of the Dome is a small but fascinating museum of sports memorabilia with an unwieldy official title: "The Kingdome Sports Museum Featuring the Royal Brougham Collection." The collection's name is taken from a legendary sports reporter and longtime editor of the *Seattle Post-Intelligencer.* Brougham died after suffering a heart attack in the Kingdome press box in 1978.

The collection actually began in 1976, when Brougham contacted the Kingdome organizers to say that he had an office so full of memorabilia that he could barely move. Would they be interested in some of it? The answer was yes. Since then, many others have donated to the collection—including local restaurateur and baseball fan Bill Gasparetti. Some of the items are old, such as a blackened baseball—used in Kansas on the 4th of July, 1886—and a football faceguard dating from 1891. Some are part of local history: a bat autographed by 1920s Seattle players, a football from the 1919 Washington-California game, and a 45rpm recording of the official team song of the late Seattle Pilots ("Go, Go, You Pilots," on Pilotune Records, performed by Doris Doubleday and His [sic] Command Pilots). And some are part of more recent Seattle sports history: Steve Largent's Seahawks uniform, Lenny Wilkens's Sonics shirt, Sonny Sixkiller's jersey ("6 KILLER") from his days as the University of Washington's star quarterback.

Other items in the collection are personal relics from famous athletes. Among them are Dizzy Dean's uniform, Evel Kneivel's helmet, Muhammad Ali's autographed boxing shorts, Pele's uniform from the first public event in the Kingdome (a soccer game between the Cosmos and the Sounders), and polo mallets used by Will Rogers shortly before his fatal airplane trip with Wiley Post. There are also baseballs autographed by Babe Ruth and Hank

Seattle sportswriter Royal Brougham accepting the Silver Skis Perpetual Trophy.

Aaron, the Louisville Slugger used by Joe DiMaggio to hit safely in 56 consecutive games (a major-league record), a pair of Rocky Marciano's gloves, golfer "Babe" Didrikson Zaharias's personal harmonica, and a wood chip from the hull of the 12-meter ship *Intrepid*, winner of the 1974 America's Cup.

A wall display shows dozens of Brougham's press passes, including those from the 1936 Berlin Olympics (when Hitler snubbed African-American runner Jesse Owens in front of the world) and a number of Henley regattas.

Kingdome • 201 S King Street, Seattle, Washington 98104 • (206) 296-3124 or (206) 296-3126
Admission: Free. **Hours:** The museum is open before and after every sporting event. Kingdome tours (which include the museum) are given three times daily at 11am, 1pm, and 3pm mid-April–mid-September. Tour price is $3, with discounts for children and seniors. Group tours only mid-Sept–mid-April. **To get there:** The museum is on the arena level near Gate B, on the southwest "side" of the dome.

A Ton of Gold for a Ton of Goods

SEATTLE
Klondike Gold Rush National Historic Park

No nature trails in this park! Tucked away in one of Pioneer Square's vintage brick buildings (a space formerly housing a cookie factory and a mission), the Klondike Park is chock full of information and memorabilia from the days when Seattle was the jumping-off point for prospectors headed north to the Yukon. One hundred thousand people set out for the Klondike gold fields; 40,000 got as far as Dawson City, Alaska; about 4,000 actually found gold; roughly 300 became wealthy; and only 50 managed to keep their riches. But the Klondike's legacy brought fortune to Seattle—merchants outfitting the prospectors did $25 million in

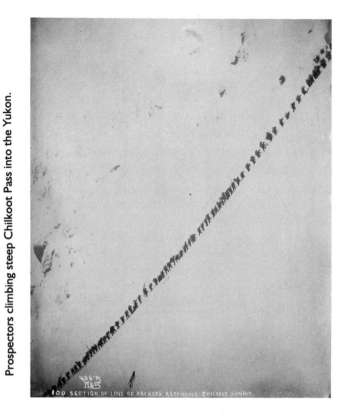

Prospectors climbing steep Chilkoot Pass into the Yukon.

trade within eight months, permanently establishing the fledgling town as the commercial center of the Northwest.

We stared in disbelief at the gear a miner had to carry: tools, cooking utensils, foodstuffs, and medicines (like Stuart's Dyspepsia Tablets), as well as clothing that would withstand temperatures from 65 degrees below zero to 95 degrees above, be impervious to ice, snow, rain, and mud, and repel man-eating Alaskan mosquitoes. Also on display: equipment for assaying gold, gold bars and nuggets, lots of early photos.

The rangers on duty certainly know their subject and, if you don't feel like exploring yourself, they schedule guided tours and gold-panning demonstrations several times a day. They also sponsor walking tours of Pioneer Square every Saturday at

1:30pm during the summer. In the small auditorium at the back of the park, a variety of films on the Gold Rush are shown daily at 3pm. Klondike, ho!

Klondike Gold Rush National Historic Park • 117 S Main Street, Seattle, Washington 98104 • (206) 553-7220
Admission: Free. **Hours:** Every day 9am–5pm; closed Thanksgiving, Christmas, and New Year's Day. **To get there:** The museum is two blocks north of the Kingdome and one and a half blocks east of the waterfront.

Good Old Trucks

SEATTLE
Last Resort Fire Department

Charlene Quan remembers her dad, Charlie Hibbert, waving to her as his fire truck roared out of the station to a fire. "It was always the second truck," she says, "so when we [kids] heard the siren, we had time to get to the window." As a young girl Quan sometimes visited her dad at the fire station, but back then, she says, the fire department was so strict that kids couldn't touch anything, climb on a fire truck, or even make any noise. Imagine Quan's joy, then, when she volunteered to help out at the Last Resort Fire Department in Ballard and saw in its collection the very same 1950 Kenworth fire truck her father had ridden. Today, as a volunteer member of the "department," she not only gets to touch the fire truck, she gets to polish it, maintain it, and drive it in parades.

Seattle fire fighter Galen Thomaier and his dad, Boyd Thomaier, started rescuing and refurbishing vintage Seattle-area fire trucks in the 1960s. Over the years they hauled trucks out of mud pits, recovered others from scrap-metal dealers, and gently negotiated with fire chiefs for precious bits of fire-fighting history, including photographs, uniforms, and street-corner fire alarm boxes. The Thomaiers' goal was to create an organization that would keep vintage, retired trucks shiny and operational, part of a "traveling museum" to be shared with the public at parades, exhibitions, and fire-prevention education events. Galen Thomaier says that "letting the public see these trucks and hear them is much more thrilling than keeping them sitting in a building somewhere."

When they're not all lined up in a Seafair parade or regional event, a dozen of the museum's trucks are tightly squeezed into the department's Ballard building, and as many are stored in garages and backyards around the region. As the collection has grown, so has the organization of fire fighters and fire truck enthusiasts who show up to help maintain the fleet and drive the trucks in community events. The collection's highlights include a 1913 Seagrave City Service ladder truck with handmade wooden ladders and an Ahrens-Fox pumper, which the Seattle Fire Department purchased new in 1927 because it had enough pumping capacity to push water to the top of the Smith Tower—at the time, the tallest building west of the Mississippi.

The members of the Last Resort Fire Department are a dedicated bunch who polish and service the vehicles regularly so that, as Boyd Thomaier used to say, "if all else fails, as a last resort you can call us to help put out a fire."

Last Resort Fire Department • 1433 NW 51st Street, Seattle, Washington 98107 • (206) 783-4474
Admission: Free. • **Hours:** By appointment only. • **To get there:** Call for directions.

A Seagrave 55-foot ladder truck, "responding since 1913."

A total of 12,571 Corsairs were built between 1938 and 1952. The plane on view at the Museum of Flight spent more than 30 years at the bottom of Lake Washington after a midair collision in 1950.

Soaring Through History

Museum of Flight

O ut-of-towners often think of Seattle as "that place where the airplanes come from." Hey, it's not for nothing that Seattle was once called "Jet City." The Museum of Flight, a world-class array of airplane paraphernalia, honors the arena that the Boeing Co. and its local offshoots have done so much to advance: the world of aviation.

This museum, located near the runway at Boeing Field, has two parts. The soaring glass-and-steel structure visible from the freeway is the immediate draw, but to set the mood you can first look back at the wild and woolly days of early aviation by starting your tour next door, in the Red Barn.

Shortly after the turn of the century, the Red Barn was Boeing's first manufacturing plant; in 1983 it reopened as a museum. The restoration retains much of the barn's original wood, so it doesn't just look good—it *smells* good. Well-presented displays hold a double cargo-bay's worth of information guaranteed to interest both adults and kids. Some sample fun facts:

• The world's first daily commercial route, begun in 1914 between Tampa and St. Petersburg, Florida, carried one passenger at a time.

• The first Alaskan airmail delivery (Fairbanks to McGrath, in 1924) took three hours. By dogsled, the same route took 17 days.

• During a financial slump in the aviation market between the wars, Boeing tried its hand at furniture making. On display is a sample Boeing Chiffonette, a chest of drawers that is probably best described as sturdily utilitarian. For a furniture designer, the Boeing Co. makes great airplanes.

Also in the barn are working early airplane engines, a model of the Wright Brothers' wind tunnel, and a beautifully restored Curtiss Robin. The Curtiss Robin is the plane that Wrong-Way Corrigan "accidentally" flew from New York to Ireland in 1938. After being refused permission to fly across the Atlantic, Corrigan filed a flight plan to follow the coast south; later, when he landed in Ireland, he claimed he'd gotten mixed up in the heavy fog. A life-size blowup of old Corrigan himself leans jauntily against the museum's Robin.

If the Red Barn grounds us in the pioneer days of flight, the Great Gallery shoots us into the present and future. Flying, as Wilbur and his brother would tell you, isn't just history; it's hardware. And that means planes, lots of them—43 of them here, with over 50 more awaiting restoration. Airplane nuts, uninterested family members, kids, and everyone in between can get up close and personal with these planes, which have been carefully restored by volunteers, many of whom are retired Boeing workers and engineers. Among them are a B-17 Flying Fortress (actually, outside—that is, when it's not starring in a movie), a Voight Crusader, a 1929 80A Boeing trimotor (the only one still in existence), a fragile Czech glider, a Kaydet (the famous biplane trainer), a McDonnell Douglas A4F once used by the Blue Angels, and a bizarre gyrocopter that looks like an overgrown eggbeater.

The museum also displays an improbable flying automobile called the Aerocar, invented in the late 1940s by Molt Taylor of Longview, Washington. The Aerocar, one of the museum's most popular attractions, was designed to beat traffic jams: it had wings and a rear propeller that could be detached and towed when the vehicle was used as a car, then reattached when you wanted to get away from it all. As of this writing the Aerocar was on display at Sea-Tac International Airport, but it will eventually return to the Museum of Flight.

Another of the museum's most popular rare planes is the A12 Blackbird, a sleek and once-top-secret Lockheed production that has only recently become declassified. The Blackbird holds both the world's absolute speed record (2,242.48mph) and the world's absolute altitude record (85,069 feet). Just to give you an idea of how fast this baby flies, it'll go coast to coast in 67 minutes, or New York to London in just under two hours. The Museum of Flight had been on a waiting list for several years when the Blackbird was declassified in 1990; five models went to NASA and one came here.

Kids will enjoy climbing in the cockpit of a full-scale mockup of an F-18 fighter, as well as the weekend educational programs on everything from jets to rockets to model-building. The museum also has a small but good reference library, currently open on Tuesdays or by appointment, and a theater for aviation-related films and other public programs.

NOTE: Another flight museum is in the works, at the tiny airport in McMinnville, Oregon. Wealthy entrepreneur Delford Smith is currently assembling a huge collection of historic airplanes for his Evergreen AirVenture Museum. Among them is the *Spruce Goose*, the famous 140-ton wooden "flying boat" built by Howard Hughes.

Museum of Flight • 9404 E Marginal Way, Tukwila, Washington 98108 • (206) 764-5720
Admission: $5 for adults, discounts for children. **Hours:** Every day 10am–5pm, Thurs 10am–9pm; closed Christmas. **To get there:** Take exit 158 from I-5 and follow the signs; at the light (E Marginal Way S), go right; the museum is about 1 mile up E Marginal Way S.

Bobo's Back

The B-1 flying boat built in 1919 was the first commercial aircraft designed, engineered, and constructed by the Boeing Co., back when fewer than 100 people worked for Bill Boeing. Only one B-1 was built; it was used for the first regular international airmail run between Seattle and Victoria from 1920 to 1927, and racked up a record-breaking 350,000 air miles.

The open cockpit, wooden-hulled biplane was purchased by the Seattle Historical Society in 1942 for a few hundred dollars and restored to its original condition. At its unveiling in 1951, C. L. Egtvedt, who was the B-1's chief design engineer and copilot for its maiden voyage over Lake Union, reminisced: "That was quite an airplane in its day, but there were still a number of skeptics around the shop before we got into the air . . . One of the foremen even offered to bet Bill Boeing that it would never get off the water. [After takeoff] we skimmed over the tops of some anchored boats in a series of upward swoops and dives. The crowd watching from the shore got pretty nervous before we landed, I understand—but not half as nervous as we were."

Today the B-1 is probably the single most important artifact at the Museum of History and Industry. Chief curator Sheryl Stiefel calls it "our icon." Yet, hanging above the descending rampway, it is almost hidden. Be sure to look up—it's easy to miss.

After craning your neck for the B-1, make your way through MOHAI's other exhibits that tell the story of Seattle. Among our favorites: one of the famous locally designed and built Slo-Mo hydroplanes, the Iron Chink (a mechanized salmon-gutter that revolutionized the canning industry), a wax diorama of the landing at Alki Point by the first white settlers in Seattle, and an immense detailed painting by Rudolf Zallinger of the 1889 Great Seattle Fire.

Recently discovered amid a pile of other artifacts (but not yet on display): a spool of genuine red tape. Red cotton twill tape was once used by the U.S. government to bind official documents for storage in vertical files; the museum's sample (now faded to pale pink) came from the Port of Seattle customhouse at the turn of the century.

We applaud MOHAI's recent decision to present a number of pop culture–oriented artifacts alongside more traditional stuff. For instance, the preserved body of Woodland Park Zoo's most famous gorilla is now on permanent display after an absence of several years. Bobo's back!

A hidden bonus lurks for the mildly adventurous. A huge cross-section of a Douglas fir, with rings marked by small plaques that show the years from A.D. 1177 to 1947, is located under the ramp at the back of the museum.

Museum of History and Industry • 2700 24th Avenue E, Seattle, WA 90112 • (206) 324-1175
Admission: $3 for adults, discounts for children and senior citizens. **Hours:** Every day 10am–5pm. **To get there:** Traveling east on SR 520, take the Montlake Boulevard exit. Stay in the right lane. Go through intersection and turn left on 24th Avenue. Traveling west on SR 520, take the Lake Washington Boulevard exit. Turn right at the stop sign. Drive ¼ mile and turn right on 24th Avenue.

A Museum That Defies Description

SEATTLE
New Museum of Hysteria and Indecision

Here's artist Michael Murphy explaining how his studio became a museum: "We kept getting crowds from the Kingdome wanting to kill time before events. They'd wander in

here and say, 'What's all this stuff?' Also, we had a neon sign saying 'We B Art' in the window, and people would sometimes bang down the door in the middle of the night to ask if this was a bar. We decided that if people were going to come in here, they might as well pay for it, so we started charging two bucks for a tour. Whenever anyone asked if it was worth it, we'd always say, 'No!'—but people kept coming anyway."

The New Museum of Hysteria and Indecision is a real combo plate: part fencing academy, part art gallery, part studio. Tours are a must here, because there are few guideposts. In between piles of welding equipment, masks from around the world, and half-finished projects are a large number of more-or-less conventional artworks by Murphy and his studio mates—that is, stuff meant to be hung on the wall or set on the floor. The collection is constantly changing, but among the fairly permanent exhibits are "the ship that brought the first two artists to Earth"—a pirate ship made from an old wooden skiff, kitted out with armchairs, flags, and a Chinese lantern on top.

There are also several vehicles built for the Gravity Car Derby. This event—a face-off between artist-built soapbox racers—began in the 1970s at Post Alley, in the Public Market, and moved in successive years to Fat Tuesday and the Bumbershoot Festival. Among those on display are the fearsome Phoenix ("built for defense only"), a tanklike car with rhino horns, sliders to push opponents off-course, holes through which water is squirted, and a fire extinguisher to fog up the runway. Another car is distinguished by six seats from a renovated movie theater, mounted on a platform and steered from the back row.

Don't miss Steve Walker's beautifully restored (and much modified) 1958 Alfa Romeo Veloce race car, one of only 1,200 made. The car, which resembles a shiny, bulbous insect, has a vanity license plate that reads MUSEUM and the We B Art logo painted boldly on the front. A large advertising poster nearby continues the theme: "TIRED OF RUST AND DENTS? TRY URBAN CAMOFLAJ MOBIL MURALS. Protects and Beautifies." Several samples are shown, including a car with a painted-on parking ticket and another called the Boilerplate model ("They'll look twice before pulling out in front of this").

On one wall is a rack of sabers that Murphy, with a demonic gleam in his eye, will be happy to demonstrate. If you dare, ask him to take off his shirt and show you the tattoo on his belly of a dotted line and the word HERE.

New Museum of Hysteria and Indecision • 114 3rd Avenue S, Seattle, Washington 98104 • (206) 624-6562 or (206) 546-9794
Admission: Around $2; free tour if you buy a museum T-shirt. **Hours:** Fri 7pm–9pm, Sat–Sun 12pm–5pm; other times by appointment. **To get there:** The studio is on 3rd Avenue between Smith Tower and Pioneer Square, south of Seattle's downtown core.

Bows and Arrows

SEATTLE
The St. Charles Archery Museum

The practice of hunting with a bow and arrow has a long and rich history stretching back thousands of years and across many cultures. The bow-and-arrow combination was the most common weapon worldwide until the sixteenth century, and even since its displacement by firearms, it has remained popular for sport. A shrine to this ancient and nowadays controversial hunting method is located in a nondescript shopping center in the South Seattle suburb of Normandy Park.

Definitely not a congenial place for animal rights activists or vegetarians, the St. Charles Museum of Archery illustrates a complex world that we thought existed only in Robin Hood movies. Glenn St. Charles is an internationally recognized hunter and bow maker who founded the Pope and Young Club, the official U.S. record-keeping organization for animals taken with bow and arrow. Since the 1940s St. Charles has owned and operated the Northwest Archery Co., a specialty store stocking hundreds of esoteric tools and gadgets related to target practice and bow hunting. Several of St. Charles's children work in the store, and in 1983 the family added a large wing to make this collection available to the public.

The museum comprises a handsome set of rooms styled after a classic hunting lodge, with wood paneling, a large stone fireplace, and exposed beams. At the heart of the collection is a large group of items associated with two men who are considered gods in the world of bow hunting: Saxton Pope and Art Young. Pope was a physician at the University of California at Berkeley who treated Ishi, the last of the Yahi tribe of Northern California Native Americans. Ishi, who had walked out of the woods in 1911 to experience his first contact with Western civilization, was the subject of a classic anthropological study. Pope became his friend and mentor, and Ishi taught the surgeon to make bows and arrows and hunt with them. Pope's 1923 book on the subject, *Hunting with the Bow and Arrow*, did much to popularize the sport in America.

Five of Ishi's arrows are on display in the St. Charles collection. In the years following Ishi's death in 1916, Pope and Young traveled all over the world hunting big game, and the collection has many pieces of their tackle and memorabilia, including nine bows, a section of a moose's rib cut in half by an arrow, and an arrow

Ishi, the legendary Yahi Indian, skillfully fits arrow to bow. The last surviving member of his tribe, Ishi became the subject of a much-heralded anthropological study when he emerged from the California wilderness in 1911.

bitten in half by a lion in Africa. Along one wall of the museum are more than 200 antique wooden bows, mostly from Europe and America, intended for both target practice and hunting. So many arrowheads are on display that the St. Charleses have mounted some on the ceiling. Several of Glenn St. Charles's own creations are on display, including a bow made of yew and baleen. Baleen is the cartilagelike material found in the mouths of some whales, used for straining plankton. An unused baleen "blank" is on display next to St. Charles's bow.

Modern archery can be a very high tech sport, and flight shooting is perhaps the highest-tech of all. In this rarefied competition, accuracy is forgotten; distance is the only thing measured. Archers compete on the salt flats of the Southwest, so they have a better chance of retrieving the special needlelike graphite arrows they use. The distances traveled by the arrows are astonishing: the record for a standing archer is over 1,000 yards, while the record for a sitting archer, who braces the bow with the feet and pulls with both arms, is over a mile. Several varieties of these sophisticated bows and arrows are on display.

There's also a display case of antique bow-making tools, including a bow blank made of yew, and a reference library (the oldest book is *Essay on Archery*, dated 1792 and signed by the author,

W. M. Moseley). There are trophies, medals, and patches, a large collection of quivers (both handmade and manufactured), and a double-edged "archer's knife" from the 1920s. One end of the museum is devoted to stuffed and mounted animals—about half of them taken by Glenn St. Charles, the rest by family members or friends—including caribou, bear, mountain goats, bighorn sheep, cougar, lynx, moose, and antelope.

St. Charles Archery Museum, Northwest Archery Co. • 19807 1st **Avenue S, Seattle, Washington 98148** • **(206) 878-7300**
Admission: Free. Hours: Tues–Wed 10am–6pm, Thurs–Fri 12pm–8pm, Sat 10am–5pm. To get there: From I-5 take exit 151 (200th Street S), continue west 2½ miles to 1st Avenue S, turn right. Northwest Archery is a half-block up on the left.

African Masks

Katherine White Collection of
African Art, Seattle Art Museum

I n 1991 the Seattle Art Museum moved from its cramped old quarters in Volunteer Park to an acclaimed new space downtown. The new building, designed by architect Robert Venturi, has quadrupled the museum's space, making available to the public many works that had previously been seen only in special exhibits.

The museum is known around the world for its collection of Asian artifacts. Less famous is the Katherine White Collection of African Art, one of the most comprehensive of its type in the United States. This assemblage—nearly 2,000 pieces—was gathered in the 1960s and 1970s by White, a pioneer collector of African textiles, decorative arts, and household objects. It has been the basis of several groundbreaking books and exhibits, including the standard reference in African art history, *African Art in Motion*, by Robert Farris Thompson.

At the collection's core is an extraordinary array of masks, sculptures, jewelry, textiles, and costumes from such tribes as the Ejagham of the Cross River Region, the Dan of Liberia, and the Yoruba of Nigeria. Arranged in three galleries, the pieces are by turns stately, terrifying, and uplifting, and they give us a glimpse into the ways that art and life combine in African culture.

NOTE: A world away from tribal life in Africa is another unusual aspect of the new museum: a high-tech computer-access digitized art kiosk called "ViewPoint." The computer's oversize monitor is touch-sensitive; press the screen and you are taken on a selective tour of the museum's holdings. With a few touches you can see multiple views of a work accompanied by a narration by its creator. Not everything in the museum is available for viewing by computer— the emphasis is on the Native American and African

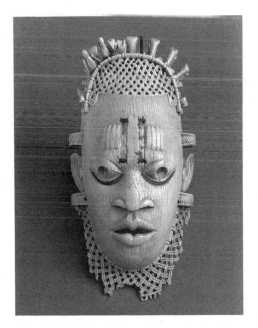

collections— and it's certainly no substitute for seeing the real thing. But ViewPoint is a fascinating look at one piece of emerging technology— and it's fun to use.

Seattle Art Museum • 100 University Street, Seattle, Washington 98101 • (206) 654-3100

Admission: $5 for adults, discounts for children and senior citizens; free on the first Tues of every month. **Hours:** Tues–Wed and Fri–Sat 10am–5pm, Thurs 10am–9pm, Sun 12pm–5pm. **To get there:** The museum is two blocks south of the Pike Place Market, with entrances on 1st and 2nd avenues.

Little Black Sambo Revisited

SEATTLE
African-American Children's Books, Seattle Public Library

The 7,000 volumes in the African-American Reading Room in the Douglass-Truth branch of the Seattle Public Library include a number of subgroups, among them art, politics, and music. One of the most interesting is a 500-plus–volume collection of children's books that reveal how African-Americans have been portrayed in children's literature throughout the years.

The material is by turns patronizing, disturbing, amusing, and enlightening. It runs the gamut from a turn-of-the-century copy of *The Story of Little Black Sambo* by Helen Bannerman to picture books by Ezra Jack Keats, and other contemporary authors. *King Tom and the Runaways: The Story of What Befell Two Boys in a Georgia Swamp*, by Louis Pendleton (which bears the inscription "Jason from Grandpapa Xmas 1890"), is set in 1855; the narrative describes a slave named Jim as being "above the average of his race in intelligence and sagacity." This dated writing contrasts with modern material more suited to contemporary sensibilities, such as the young adult novels of Walter Dean Myers or *Under the Sunday Tree*, a collection of poems by Eloise Greenfield with ebullient paintings by the Bahamian artist Amos Ferguson.

Douglass-Truth also maintains a clipping file on one of Seattle's most famous sons, Jimi Hendrix. Plans are currently under way for a major museum devoted to Hendrix, to be housed at Seattle Center at the site of the former Seattle Art Museum satellite.

Douglass-Truth Branch, Seattle Public Library • 23rd and Yesler, Seattle, Washington 98122 • (206) 684-4704
Admission: Free. **Hours:** Mon–Wed 1pm–9pm, Thurs 10am–9pm, Sat 10am–6pm, Sun 1pm–5pm. **To get there:** Douglass-Truth is in Seattle's Central District, on the corner of 23rd Street and Yesler Way.

A Treasury of John Hancocks

SEATTLE
Autograph Collection, Seattle Public Library

Most library autograph collections end up in cardboard boxes that are inaccessible to anyone but scholars. Lucky for us, the Albert Balch Autograph Collection at the Seattle Public Library's main branch downtown is the only library-owned autograph collection in the United States that is staffed and accessible to the general public.

Albert Balch was a prominent Seattle-area realtor, land developer, and civic booster. He was also an enthusiastic autograph collector, having begun his collection while growing up on a farm near the Canadian border. When Peace Arch Park on the U.S.-Canadian border was dedicated in Blaine after the First World War, a number of dignitaries, including Marshal Foch, attended the

LEAPIN' LIZARDS! LOOKIE, SANDY - ISN'T THAT OUR GOOD FRIEND, AL BALCH?

ARF!

HAROLD GRAY ■

ceremonies. "As far as I can tell, that was Albert Balch's first school-boy autograph-collecting experience," says Paul Feavel, the coordinator of the Balch Collection.

Over the years, Balch corresponded with people throughout the world, banged on the doors of local leaders, and buttonholed prominent visitors to the Northwest. In the early 1940s he offered the resulting collection to the Seattle Public Library for display in exchange for help with keeping it current. After Balch's death in the 1970s, the collection became the property of the library; his will also provided funds for a curator and an operating budget.

Curator Feavel spends his days, he says, "wading through sixty-some years of things thrown in boxes." He is now nearing the end of his Herculean task: putting autographs into acid-free archival sleeves, making safety photocopies, devising cross-referenced indexes, and performing detective work on the many unidentified or indecipherable items. He has also sent out requests for new material, which he plans to pursue more aggressively once the cataloguing is complete. The collection now has 7,000 to 8,000 items.

The range of Balch's collection is, to say the least, eclectic. Edward Teller, the "father" of the atomic bomb, provided a special statement about his hopes for the future of atomic energy. Benito Mussolini sent an official state photo, signed and sealed. (When Balch requested material from Il Duce, he was visited by an Italian Secret Service officer who wanted to know his reasons; Balch showed him his collection, and a few weeks later the photo arrived.) Balch also collected the John Hancocks of Emma Goldman, Mother Jones, Eleanor Roosevelt, Jimmy Hoffa, Emperor Hirohito, Grace Kelly, the Shah of Iran, Jane Addams, Prince Sihanouk, Whoopi Goldberg, and Kings Edward VIII and George III.

Balch apparently had a soft spot for cartoonists. Among those represented are Milt Caniff ("Terry and the Pirates"), Chester Gould ("Dick Tracy"), Harold Gray ("Little Orphan Annie"), Garry Trudeau ("Doonesbury"). Many supplied original artwork or sketches made especially for the collection. "There's also a Walt Disney," Feavel says, "but I need to do some checking on that one. Disney actually signed very few of his autographs; he had people who signed and did sketches for him, and I think this may be one of those."

The Balch collection is housed in an employees-only area of the downtown library, but books of photocopies are available

Love, Suffer and Work.

(Aimer, Travailler et Souffrir.)

for casual browsing, and Feavel is available by appointment for consultation on specific items or to authenticate or evaluate autographs.

Seattle Public Library • 1000 4th Avenue, Seattle, Washington 98104 • (206) 386-4670
Admission: Free. **Hours:** Mon–Thurs 9am–9pm, Fri–Sat 9am–6pm, Sun 1pm–5pm; consultation available by appointment. **To get there:** The Seattle Public Library's main branch is between 4th and 5th avenues and Spring and Madison streets in downtown Seattle.

Majestic MIGHTY MONARCH *of the* AIR

Superheterodyne
RADIO

Gathered 'Round the Radio

Majestic Model 307

SEATTLE
Shoreline Community Museum

For years, radio was America's primary link to news, culture, and entertainment. It warmed our hearts, scared us, kept us current. Return with us now to those thrilling days of Jack Benny, FDR's fireside chats, and the Brooklyn Dodgers.

The Shoreline Community Museum has a collection of vintage radios to show off in style. A mishmash of vintage radio shows—news, soap operas, ads, music—begins playing when you walk into the large room where the Puget Sound Antique Radio

Association has assembled several dozen radios and TVs. The radios are arranged by decade and each has a brief explanatory note. There's a hands-on telegraph for kids; assorted radio parts and accessories; the first commercial magnetic tape recorder, made in the 1940s by the Brush Corp. of Cleveland; and vintage advertisements praising the new technology ("It's new . . . it's breathtaking . . . it's black magic"). An all-wood, 1930s-era tube-tester looks more like your grandmother's chest of drawers than an electronic gadget.

Want to hem a skirt or mend a shirt button while listening to the wireless? The Shoreline Museum also has an extensive collection of sewing memorabilia, originally collected by the Pacific Northwest Needle Art Guild (PANNAG). Among the artifacts from the early 1800s to the present, thimbles alone account for over 500 pieces: you've got your advertising thimbles, your thimbles in animal shapes (ceramic bunnies are well represented), your thimble keychains, and your thimbles of such unusual materials as abalone shell.

You can browse through several hundred needle holders, pin-cushions in more shapes than you thought imaginable, punches, chatelaines, bodkins, crochet hooks, darning needles, sewing baskets, embroidery hoops, spool holders, irons, crimping machines, sewing machines, egg darners, and military and travel sewing kits. Look for real oddities among the ordinary, such as the Victorian-era black pins and needles (for use while in mourning) and the combination pincushion/tape measures. One of these looks like a gold and jewel-encrusted coffee grinder (crank the handle to wind the tape in).

Shoreline Community Museum • 749 N 175th Street, Seattle, Washington 98133 • (206) 542-7111
Admission: Free, donations accepted. **Hours:** Tues–Sat 10am–4pm. **To get there:** From I-5, take the 175th Street/Aurora exit westbound. The museum is on the south side of 175th Street, east of Aurora.

40,000 Jars of Pickled Fish

SEATTLE: UNIVERSITY OF WASHINGTON
Fisheries Department

The 40,000 jars of preserved fish in the U.W. Fisheries Department collection represent about half the total number of North Pacific marine species. The collection is unique in its focus and is considered one of the more important regional research collections of its type in the United States.

The samples are initially preserved in formaldehyde and maintained in 70 percent ethanol. According to collections manager Lex Snyder, specimens can last for hundreds of years under proper conditions. Marine samples collected over 200 years ago by Captain Cook, for example, remain in excellent condition at London's British Museum. The fish are stored in labeled glass jars and kept in a large, climate- and light-controlled room in the basement of the Fisheries Teaching and Research (FTR) Building, at the south end of the University of Washington campus.

The collection is arranged phylogenetically—that is, by evolutionary relationship. It begins with lampreys, which are relatively primitive in structure, and ends with samples of blowfish and flatfish, whose characteristics are considered to be more advanced.

Compare the wrasses, tiny coral-reef dwellers with pretty, poochy mouths, to the aptly named blob sculpin, a deep-water fish (its home is at about 900 meters) that tends toward the grotesque. The sculpin has only primitive eyes, but its sensitive "hair" (actually, fleshy protrusions called cirri) detects the movement of its prey. The largest fish in the collection is a 9-foot-long, six-gilled shark that weighed over 200 pounds when it was caught by two men trolling for salmon near Everett. It requires a custom tank for storage.

The fish collection is not normally open to the public, but Snyder, the collection's sole staff member, will conduct school group

tours by appointment. She is also available to answer specific questions involving such problems as species or fossil identification.

If you visit the Fisheries Building, don't miss the lobby display of sand collected from all over the world by graduate students. There are samples from the Marshall Islands, Nevada, Oroville, Ayers Rock, and other locales.

NOTE: A short walk away, adjacent to the University Bookstore branch (second floor of the east wing of the South Campus Center), is a stained-glass window depicting George Washington with the Latin inscription *Num, me vexo?* It was several years after the building was completed before the phrase was made public. It's a translation of "What, me worry?"—which anyone who grew up reading *Mad* magazine will recognize as the immortal motto of Alfred E. Neuman, *Mad*'s mascot.

Fisheries Teaching and Research Building • 1140 NE Boat Street, University of Washington HF15, Seattle 98195 • (206) 543-3816

Admission: Free. **Hours:** By appointment only. **To get there:** Boat Street runs along the north edge of Portage Bay. The Fisheries Building is west of the University Hospital complex.

Mourning Bodices and Pre-Columbian Cloth

SEATTLE: UNIVERSITY OF WASHINGTON
Henry Art Gallery Costume and Textile Collection

The 15,500 pieces in the textile and costume collection of the Henry Art Gallery at the University of Washington represent hand-woven and hand-decorated textiles from all over the world. Over 1,000 people a year—mainly teachers, historians, students, ethnographers, designers, and weavers—conduct research here. (Curator Judy Sourakli stresses that anyone making an appointment must have legitimate research questions.)

A late nineteenth-century utility cloth, called a *kantha*, from Bangladesh.

The collection includes functional textiles, ceremonial clothing, shoes, hats, and accessories from virtually every continent and era—from a fragment of Egyptian cloth, circa 1500 B.C., to a pair of funky sandals, circa late 1970s, that double as roller skates. (Imagine Birkenstock-style sandals with thick platform soles; pull a lever and presto—miniature wheels drop out of recesses in the soles.)

Other items include a piece of pre-Columbian Peruvian cloth from the eleventh or twelfth century; children's clothing, including some rare mourning bodices; high-fashion dresses and shoes from contemporary designers; woven fragments from the Coptic culture of the fifth or sixth century; elaborately detailed 1870s-era American wedding dresses; and a small but significant amount of men's clothing. Some pieces are utilitarian, others decorative; some combine function with beauty, such as a rare woven silk floor cloth, made in Syria in the 19th century and used for sitting on the floor while eating.

A tapestry of historical, anthropological, and socioeconomic information can be found by examining a single subcollection. A geographic cross section of traditional Indian clothing, for instance, makes it clear that each region and town has a distinctive "uniform," a style of clothing that may differ in tiny ways from that of other regions but that serves to make a person's identity clear. A look at the same items across time shows that changes in such traditional styles occur very slowly, in contrast with the blinding speed of modern fashion.

Elaborate measures are taken to ensure that specimens remain intact. The collection's rooms are dust-free and temperature- and light-controlled; study is done with the aid of gloves and cloth covers in the collection's research labs.

A research trip to the collection is usually a two-day process—one day to use the in-depth catalogue and determine exactly which items are needed, another to view the pieces themselves. However, if time permits, the staff will try to accommodate the needs of out-of-town users in a single day.

Costume and Textile Collection, Henry Art Gallery • Chemistry
Library Building, University of Washington DE-15, Seattle, Washing-
ton 98195 • (206) 543-2281 or (206) 543-1739
Admission: Free. **Hours:** Tues–Fri 9am–5pm, by appointment only. **To get there:**
The collection is in temporary quarters on the second floor of the Chemistry Library
Building, south of the Henry Art Gallery at 15th Avenue NE and NE 41st Street.
Enter the campus at the west entrance on 15th Avenue NE.

Party Ice

SEATTLE: UNIVERSITY OF WASHINGTON
Quaternary Research Center

Quaternary" refers to the geologic period from the end of the
Tertiary period to the present—that is, the most recent of
the geologic periods. Depending on who's counting, it
stretches from today backwards to 600,000 or even 2 million
years ago.

Dr. Piet Grootes and his colleagues use sophisticated equipment to bore into glaciers in Greenland, Antarctica, and other
frozen locations, remove cylindrical samples of the ancient ice, and
bring them back for study. The samples reveal many things; for example, the characteristics of ancient atmospheres can be reconstructed from an examination of oxygen isotopes extracted from
the air bubbles trapped in the ice.

Dr. Grootes has anywhere from 5,000 to 10,000 ice samples at a given time—about as many as can be analyzed in a year.
The "cold rooms"—two large lockers that seem small because

they're crammed to overflowing with boxes of samples—are kept at 45 degrees below zero Centigrade. (Visitors are well advised to borrow the big sub-zero parkas Dr. Grootes keeps on hand.)

The organization of the rooms may seem haphazard—there are insulated boxes strewn every which way—but in fact each sample is meticulously marked. Here, for instance, is a piece of 500-year-old ice from Greenland: a cylinder of ordinary-looking ice, several feet long and about 4 inches in diameter. It is wrapped in plastic and stored in a cardboard tube with an aluminum outer coating. The date and location of the sampling are noted, along with other relevant data. But what's this? Someone has written "Party Ice" on the plastic! This, Dr. Grootes explains, is a bit of glacial humor. When ice is extracted from a glacier—from as deep as 3,000 meters below the surface—the bubbles of air trapped in the sample are compressed as much as 12 or 13 times the normal atmospheric pressure. When the ice is later melted for analysis, the bubbles make a distinct popping sound. ("Very good for ice cubes," Dr. Grootes says with a smile.) Needless to say, this stuff is hardly the sort of thing you'd really use to chill a mint julep. By the time the costs of research are added up—sending a team of scientists to a remote glacier, keeping them alive on the ice while extracting ice cores, and keeping the samples properly refrigerated during shipment, much less the actual analysis—you've got one very expensive piece of ice. Quips Dr. Grootes: "It might as well be gold."

NOTE: Dr. Grootes stresses that his collection is located in a highly specialized research facility staffed by a few busy people. Tours will be conducted only for specific purposes and must be arranged in advance.

Quaternary Research Center, Johnson Hall • University of Washington AK-60, Seattle, Washington 98195 • (206) 543-1166
Admission: Free. **Hours:** By appointment only. **To get there:** Enter the University of Washington campus from the west entrance on 15th Avenue NE. You will be given directions at the gate.

The Secrets of Telephones

Vintage Telephone Equipment Museum

Across the street from the Hat & Boots, a gas station in the shape of a giant set of cowboy hat and boots (a classic roadside attraction, now sadly abandoned), is US West's main switching station for south Seattle. Three of the floors in the station are devoted to the Vintage Telephone Equipment Museum, a massive collection that traces telephonic history from the earliest Watson-come-here models to the most thoroughly modern fiber optics.

Longtime employees of US West are called "Pioneers"; and curator Don Ostrand is one of several Pioneers who donate their time to the ongoing process of organizing the collection. It's a bewildering jumble of equipment, largely unmarked and indecipherable to the untrained eye; but with an expert like Ostrand along, the collection comes alive.

A major part of the collection is a series of working switching stations that shows the evolution of call routing—how your call is hooked up with the party you want to reach. The earliest working system on display dates from 1923 and was used when Seattle's Rainier Valley neighborhood converted from manual phones to a dial tone.

Among the museum's other highlights: a 100-line switching office originally used on the battleship *California* before the Second World War; a huge ceramic microphone that hung around the neck of an early switchboard operator (good neck muscles were a must); noisily clacking teletype machines, circa 1930; a Wheatstone Perforator, which punched type for the automatic transmission of Morse code; a Western Union Desk-Fax, probably dating from the 1950s; and a 1960s-era data test center from the early days of computer data transmission.

Compare phone styles through the years—from early models with cranks and no dials to Picture-Phones from the 1962 World's Fair, to modern touch-tones. Ostrand says that children are often stymied by the old-fashioned rotary phones on display—they keep trying to punch the buttons.

Ever wonder what goes on in those cocoonlike canvas tents on telephone poles? Displays reveal the inner workings of outdoor aboveground and underground repair. Last but not least is a fine collection of slugs—not the squishy kind, but fake coins used to make free calls.

Vintage Telephone Equipment Museum • 7000 E Marginal Way S, Seattle, Washington 98106 • (206) 767-3012 or (206) 789-4761

Admission: By donation. **Hours:** Tues 8am–2:30pm; other times by appointment. **To get there:** From I-5, take the Michigan/Corson Street exit. Take Corson to E Marginal Way. The three-story aggregate building is on the corner of Corson and E Marginal Way S. There's no sign—the museum entrance is on the south side.

He Just Kept Building

SEATTLE
Walker Rock Garden

Florence Walker is in her eighties and doesn't get around quickly, but she's happy to give you a partial tour of her backyard and then let you wander around on your own. It's not just any old backyard, either. It's a remarkable work of folk art— Seattle's answer to the Watts Towers of Los Angeles. It's also a testament to the singular vision of Florence's late husband, Milton, whom veteran Seattle newspaperman Emmett Watson has called "some kind of genius."

Florence and Milton Walker moved into their modest West Seattle house in 1939. For 30 years Milton was a mechanic at Boeing, and for much of that time the double yard was primarily a playground for their three children. Milton always liked to build things, and in 1954, when the last of the Walker kids finished high school, he began to build in earnest. When he retired in 1970, he built even more—and kept on building until his death in 1984.

Milton had no art training, but he began to sculpt his backyard as if it were a huge piece of Carrara marble. He built intricate fountains inlaid with colorful pieces of glass, stone, and agate. He built stone arches large and small. He enshrined pieces of lava from Idaho's Mountains of the Moon. He built obelisks, curved walls, and a system of artificial lakes and streams running through mountains made of textured basalt from Wenatchee.

During a Boeing strike in 1948, he built a massive fireplace made of small, rounded stones he and the family had collected on

beaches. He built hidden grottos, steps with butterfly-shaped stones, and a wavy concrete monolith with inlaid mosaics of wine glasses, faces, and butterflies. He built benches and walkways with gorgeous agates, many of them with recognizable shapes—here a cat or a dog, there a woman. ("Milton used to call that one his girlfriend.") All have been polished by countless backs leaning against them and countless shoes scuffing them. In honor of the nation's bicentennial, he built an elaborate, multi-tiered tower of colored glass and concrete.

"They say that the tower looks Byzantine," Florence says, "but believe me, Milton wasn't copying anything. Everything you see is pure Milton Walker. He never had any training, and he never figured things out beforehand—he just shaped it as he worked on it. He never thought of himself as an artist; I don't think anyone was as surprised as he was when he started doing this. Once the ideas came, though, he just couldn't keep up with them."

These days, about 300 people a year visit the Walker Rock Garden and sign Florence's guestbook. A few years ago, a group of Seattle-area artists formed the Friends of the Walker Rock Garden, which works to raise money for its preservation and maintenance—especially since Florence can no longer care for the many trees, flowers, and shrubs growing among the sculptures. "People always ask me what's going to happen to it when I'm gone," Florence says. "Well, there's your answer, I guess."

Walker Rock Garden • 5407 37th Avenue SW, Seattle, Washington 98116 • (206) 935-3036
Admission: By donation. **Hours:** By appointment only; closed in the winter. **To get there:** Call for directions.

The County Bells

SEATTLE
Washington State Centennial Bell Garden

The "bell garden" at the Washington State Convention & Trade Center was conceived and executed by Seattle composer David Mahler for the state's centennial celebration in 1989. Mahler was given one bell by each of the state's 39 counties. Although some were cast especially for this project, most have historical significance. They are vivid reminders of a time when the sound of a bell could be heard for miles over country roads, when bells played an important part in the state's logging, railroad, and maritime industries, and when schools and churches used bells to assemble their flocks.

Mahler heard bells often as a child in suburban Chicago, but missed them when he moved to this region. "The Pacific Northwest is young in many respects, including bells. People back East have a longer tradition that goes back to the use of bells in European schools and churches. In the Southwest they have the mission-bell tradition brought over from Spain. The oldest bell in the U.S., in fact, is in a New Mexico mission." Mahler tracked down the most interesting or significant bells he could find—a five-year process that culminated in the collection's dedication in November 1989.

Most of the bells are still in working order, and a computer system devised by Mahler has turned them into a charming musical instrument. Those bells that can still make a significant sound—28 of the 39—hang in clusters above a 350-foot stretch of walkway on the north side of the Convention Center. A computer system connects them, and each bell has a special clapper triggered by an electromagnetic switch.

The collection includes church bells, school bells, locomotive bells (especially from logging trains), nautical bells, and bells that have served multiple purposes: first as a farm bell, for instance, then a fire bell or a church bell. Whatcom County's bell was once rung by hand from the top of a building in Bellingham to help ships find their way in heavy fog. The biggest bell in the collection dates from 1878, came to Cashmere in Chelan County from Denmark, and weighs in at 600 pounds.

Mahler's personal favorite comes from Whitman County. At the turn of the century, it hung in the belfry of the Baptist church in the town of Hay—a once-thriving farming community that now has only about two dozen residents. Mahler says, "It's a town that once had a strong population, but it won't exist in another 20 years. If you look at the old railroad timetables, you can see that it used to have a lot of locomotive traffic, but the last train out— a freight train—left 15 or 20 years ago. This bell is a memorial to that town, and to the notion that things change."

Bells that are too small, damaged, or fragile to be mounted outside are displayed inside the Convention Center. Among them are a large decorative glass bell by Pilchuck glass artist William Morris, a cowbell from the Okanogan, a bell from Island County that once saw service on a ferry used as a rumrunner, and a sheep bell from Grant County.

Washington State Convention & Trade Center • 800 Convention Place, Seattle, Washington 98101 • (206) 447-5000
Admission: Free. **Hours:** Outdoors: 24 hours; indoors: every day 7am–11pm. Ringing times: every hour 10am–6pm daily, two bells are chosen randomly by a computer program to mark the hour. A "roll call" of each bell peals out at 10:30am, 5pm, and 6pm daily. Short pieces written by a variety of composers are rung at eight-minute intervals, daily 12pm–1pm and 5pm–6pm. **To get there:** From I-5 south take the Madison Street exit and follow the signs. From I-5 north, take Union Street exit, turn right at 7th Avenue, then right to Pike, and right on 8th. Parking is underground.

A Pan-Asian Experience

SEATTLE
Wing Luke Asian Museum

Asian-Americans have a long history in Seattle. The first Asians to arrive in the area were probably native Hawaiians who served as navigators for Captain Cook. Chinese immigrants became an important part of the city during the building of the railroads; a large influx of Japanese immigrants came soon after. Since that time, numerous other Asian groups have made Seattle their home.

The Wing Luke is the only pan-Asian museum in the United States. Curator Ron Chew points out that this reflects Seattle's International District's status as the only pan-Asian community in the country, where various ethnic groups mix together instead of splitting geographically into "Chinatowns," "Japantowns, "Korea-towns," and so on.

The museum is named for Wing Luke, a beloved member of Seattle's Chinese-American community and the city's first Asian-American City Councilmember. When he died in an airplane crash in the Cascades in 1965, the community contributed money to go toward the recovery of his body. But the remains of Luke and his companions were not found for several years, and the money went unspent. When his body was finally found in 1968, the community decided to use the funds to create a museum in Luke's honor.

The handsome Wing Luke Asian Museum, housed in Seattle's International District, was formerly a garage/auto shop where many Japanese-Americans left their cars when they were sent to internment camps during the Second World War. Most of the artifacts on display have been culled from the personal memorabilia of local residents. Recently the museum's entire 3,000 square feet of exhibition space was taken up by a history of the Japanese-American community during the 50 years before and after their wartime imprisonment at Camp Minidoka in Idaho. Photos, replicas of internment camp newspapers, and other displays detailed the events surrounding the infamous Executive Order 9066 of 1942 that created the camps.

Particularly instructive (and particularly chilling) were the artifacts brought back from Camp Minidoka. The "rock of ages," an ordinary stone polished on a concrete floor and burnished with an Army blanket to a high gloss, showed how detainees kept enforced idleness from crushing them. One entire room of a Minidoka cabin was replicated from the community's collective

The Amano family with Mr. Mimbu on an outing in October 1921.

memory and furnished with blankets, tins of food, even a potbelly stove brought all the way home for remembrance.

Wing Luke Asian Museum • 407 7th Avenue S, Seattle, Washington 98104 • (206) 623-5124
Admission: $2.50 for adults, discounts for children and senior citizens. **Hours:** Tues–Fri 11am–4:30pm, Sat–Sun 12pm–4pm, first Thurs of the month 11am–7pm. **To get there:** The museum is in the heart of Seattle's International District. From I-5 north, take the James/Cherry Street exit; from the south, take the Dearborn Street exit. The museum is just off the corner of 7th Avenue S and Jackson Street.

Funk 'n' Junk

SEATTLE
Ye Olde Curiosity Shop

Sometimes, making the distinction between the funky and the junky, between good bad taste and bad bad taste, is a close call. Ye Olde Curiosity Shop, on Seattle's waterfront, leans toward the latter. It is still something of a kick, but it's a pale shadow of its former funky self. Those of us who grew up in the Northwest remember the Curiosity Shop when it was genuinely eccentric and more than a little spooky. The emphasis now is more on touristy gimcracks. Still, if you've got a hankering to see Sylvester "the desert mystery" mummy and his female counterpart, Sylvia, this is the place. Other suitably bizarre relics from the shop's past glory: a chain carved from a single matchstick; a cloth "woven by his toes by an armless Mexican, Mexico City"; intimate parts of a whale's anatomy; a 6½-pound copper coin from Sweden, dated 1719; and a preserved pig, born in 1944 in East Selah, Washington, with eight legs, three eyes, three mouths, two tails, two noses, and two ears.

Ye Olde Curiosity Shop • 1001 Alaskan Way, Seattle, Washington
98104 • (206) 682-5844
Admission: Free. Hours: Sun–Thurs 9:30am–6pm, Fri–Sat 9am–9pm. To get
there: Located on Pier 54 (the same pier as Ivar's Restaurant), on Seattle's waterfront.

A tooth from a mastodon
unearthed in the early 1970s.
The tooth is estimated to be
12,000 years old.

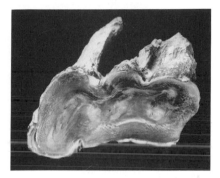

The Manis Mastodon

Museum and Arts Center

The volunteer on duty the day we visited Sequim's Museum and Arts Center admitted that without the town's one claim to fame, this would be a standard historical museum documenting the area's industries, pioneer families, and Native American heritage. But thanks to Clare and Emanual "Manny" Manis, the museum owns the tusks, ribs, toe bones, and other evidence of what's now known as the Manis Mastodon.

In 1977 the Manis family decided they needed a pond for their livestock. Manny got a backhoe and started digging in a low spot on his land. To his surprise, the tree limbs he dug up turned out be mastodon tusks. The livestock never did get their pond, because over the next nine years archaeologists working at the site found evidence of four mastodons, several bison, and tools made out of stone and wood, all dating back about 12,000 years.

Until the pits were filled in 1986, more than 20,000 people visited the dig. Today you can learn the story of the mastodon, touch one of the 12,000-year-old ribs, and learn about the archaeological dig in this unlikely spot. One tusk is kept in a metal bathtub, and pieces of mastodon kneecaps, vertebrae, and jaws are on display.

Museum and Arts Center • 175 W Cedar Street, PO Box 1002, Sequim, Washington 98382 • (206) 683-8110
Admission: By donation. **Hours:** Every day 9am–4pm; closed holidays. **To get there:** The museum is one block north of US 101 between N Sequim and 2nd avenues.

Sally Bags

SPOKANE
Cheney Cowles Museum

Kids will love this historical museum, which has lots of colorful hands-on and interactive displays. They can peer through a magnifying glass at lead and silver from 20 different area mines, feel a mink pelt, and imitate the twining technique used by Plateau Indians in making "corn husk" and "Sally" bags.

Many of the displays have recorded narrations, and in a section called "Breakthroughs in Time" visitors are treated to a vintage electric automobile, a waffle iron, an electric fan, curling irons, and early electric heaters and toasters that even seniors may have trouble identifying.

Admission to the Cheney Cowles Museum includes a tour of the Campbell House next door. This gorgeous house was built in 1898 and had 11 fireplaces. (Heating it during the winter took one cord of wood every 48 hours.) Much of the furniture you'll see here was sold or auctioned many years ago to area residents but eventually returned to the house for display. Volunteer guides point out details like the actual telephone that Mrs. Campbell used to call for her carriage on cold days, and the large first-floor library that doubled as the "event" room for weddings and funerals.

Cheney Cowles Museum • W 2316 1st Avenue, Spokane, Washington 99204 • (509) 456-3931

Admission: $2 for adults, discounts for children. **Hours:** Tues–Sat 10am–5pm, Sun 1pm–5pm. **To get there:** The museum is located west of downtown. From I-90, take exit 280A, go north on Walnut Street and west on 2nd Avenue. Watch for museum signs.

Bing Things

Crosbyana Room, Gonzaga University

H ere's a quick quiz on Tacoma, Washington's favorite son. Q: How many songs did Bing Crosby record during his career? A: Over 11,000.

Q: How many stars does he have on the sidewalk in front of Grauman's Chinese Theater? A: Three.

Q: How can you learn more about one of America's favorite entertainers? A: Visit the Crosbyana Room in the Crosby Library at Gonzaga University in Spokane. As Der Bingle would say: It's the truth, it's factual, everything is satisfactual.

Harry Lillis Crosby's distinctive, easygoing baritone was the vehicle for dozens of hit-parade tunes and million-sellers in a career that spanned more than 50 years. His "Road" movies with Bob Hope and Dorothy Lamour virtually invented the buddy picture, and his other films, such as *The Bells of St. Mary's* and *Going My Way* (for which he received an Academy Award) remain perennial favorites.

Bing moved to Spokane with his family when he was 3 years old, and in time attended its Catholic university. Although its most famous student dropped out shortly before graduation to pursue a career in show business, Gonzaga University awarded him an honorary degree in 1937. Bing subsequently became a supportive alumnus, contributing significantly to the funding for the library that bears his name.

In front of the library is a statue of Bing created by a local sculptor. Bing was almost as famous for his love of golf as for his singing, and he's shown leaning on one knee with a golf club beside him. Inside, on the second floor, is the Crosbyana Room— actually a meeting room with Crosby memorabilia in exhibit cases along each wall. Many of Bing's gold records and plaques are here, including awards he received for "Swinging on a Star," "The Whiffenpoof Song," and "Music to Shave By," an LP that also featured Louis Armstrong, Rosemary Clooney, and the Hi-Lo's. (According to the plaque presented to Crosby by Remington Electric Shavers, "Music to Shave By" was the biggest recording of 1959, with some 6 million copies pressed. But really now, how many copies were bought?) Also on display is his Oscar, along with sheet music and other show-biz memorabilia.

NOTE: The Bing Crosby Memorial Museum was founded in 1977, the year of Crosby's death, by a fan, Ken Twiss. Until recently, the museum was located in the restored Pantages Theater in downtown Tacoma, but remodeling has forced Twiss to put his collection in storage. Until it finds a home, Crosby fans will miss a rare treat. Twiss began collecting Crosby recordings and memorabilia during the Great Depression and has amassed some remarkable material: thousands of recordings, videos, and photos, as well as shelf upon shelf of actual "Bing things." Among the latter: the feather decoration he wore on a favorite hat, tags for his golf bag, a watch with a Bing Crosby face, blue-and-white cartons that once held Bing Crosby Brand vanilla ice cream, and a wooden table handmade by Der Bingle's grandfather.

Crosbyana Room in the Crosby Library, Gonzaga University • E 502 Boone Avenue, Spokane, Washington 99202 • (509) 328-4220
Admission: Free. **Hours:** Mon–Thurs 8am–12pm, Fri 8am–9pm, Sat 9am–9pm, Sun 11am–12pm; hours vary during holidays, semester breaks, and summer. The room is usually locked, but library staffers will give you the key for a self-guided tour. **To get there:** From downtown Spokane take Marin Avenue east to Division Street, turn left and go north on Division to Boone Avenue. Take a right on Boone.

Numchucks and Brass Knuckles

SPOKANE
Police Display, Spokane Airport

The airport contingent of Spokane's police department has assembled an arresting assortment of confiscated weapons and an impressive batch of police patches from around the world. They are mounted in glass cases in the rental-car section of the terminal.

When police officers from different cities and countries pass through Spokane, they often stop at Sgt. John Mease's office to pay a courtesy call. By trading patches with these visitors, Mease and his colleagues have built up a collection of over 1,000 patches, roughly 300 of which are on display. They come from as far away as New Zealand, China, France, Japan, Germany, and Jordan Valley, Oregon. Jordan Valley? It seems that about 15 years ago that town couldn't afford to pay its police chief, so it gave him legal authority to keep all the fines he collected. When an article in an East Coast newspaper revealed that he had collected in excess of a million dollars in a single year, the town voted to disband the police force. Its patch is shaped like a dollar bill, and it bears the slogan:

"The buck stops here." Only five were ever made, and the Spokane Airport's got one of them.

The weapons collection began about 15 years ago, according to "curator" Mease: "We just started collecting items not allowed to go on airplanes. People found out about them by word of mouth, and it seemed like everybody wanted to see them." Among the weapons on display are switchblades, daggers, gravity-fed knives, throwing stars, hand grenades, guns, numchucks, batons, and brass knuckles.

The display is available for viewing during regular airport hours, and even if Sgt. Mease isn't around (his normal shift is 7am–3pm) there's sure to be someone who can tell you more.

Spokane Airport • W 9000 Airport Drive, Spokane, Washington 99204 • (509) 624-2082
Admission: Free. Hours: Open 24 hours. To get there: The police department is directly behind the car on display in the lobby of the airport.

A Salmon-Bone Spirit Necklace

STEILACOOM
Steilacoom Tribal Cultural Center and Museum

The town of Steilacoom lays claim to several Washington "firsts": in 1854 it was the first town to be incorporated in Washington Territory; it was the site of the state's first library, brewery, courthouse, and territorial jail. The town has a village feel, with three museums within three blocks of each other.

When we visited the Steilacoom Tribal Cultural Center and Museum, tribal chairperson and museum director Joan Ortez was busy cooking in the museum's snack bar, which serves traditional Native American foods. When all the orders were ready, she wiped her hands and stepped into the museum galleries to tell us a little about the history of the Steilacoom Indians and to make sure we didn't overlook some of her favorite items in the collection.

Her grandmother Ellen LaTour had dreamed of making this museum a tribute to the Steilacoom tribe's history. La Tour didn't live to see it open in 1988, but we saw her inherited Russian trade beads from the 1850s and a cooking basket that belonged to her grandmother. Ortez pointed out a spirit necklace made from salmon vertebrae; it reveals how her ancestors honored the salmon and carried its spirit with them.

The lower level of the museum has a sand-filled container in which children are encouraged to dig for "artifacts" such as shells and buttons. A model nearby shows the layers of dirt found at one end of a pit dug by archaeologists from Fort Steilacoom Community College in 1982. The dig site was the home of the Steilacoom tribe, and fire-cracked rock at the lowest level provides some of the earliest evidence of the tribe's existence in this area.

Steilacoom Tribal Cultural Center and Museum • 1515 Lafayette
Street, PO Box 88419, Steilacoom, Washington 98388 • (206) 584-
6308
Admission: Adults $2, discounts for children and senior citizens. **Hours:** Tues–Sun
10am–4pm. **To get there:** From I-5, go west from exits 119 or 129. Follow signs
to Steilacoom. Lafayette Street is the main street in town. The Tribal Center is at
the corner of Lafayette and Pacific.

*A Rosary of
Ping-Pong Balls*

STEVENSON
Don Brown Rosary Collection,
Skamania County Museum

I f you weren't brought up counting prayers on a rosary, the custom may seem complicated and mysterious. For some people
it can become an obsession. Don Brown's fascination with
rosaries began when, as a young man, he was in an Oregon hospital with a bad case of pneumonia and noticed that the Sisters of
Mercy who were caring for him wore rosaries on their habits. He
began his rosary collection when he recovered, and devoted the
rest of his life to accumulating as many prayer beads as he could.
Through correspondence and word of mouth, news of Brown's
collection spread worldwide and rosaries would often show up

unsolicited at his home. By the time Brown died in 1975, the collection had grown to almost 4,000, and today it remains the largest collection of rosaries in the world.

Traditional rosaries in the Western church are made up of five sets, or decades, of ten beads each, and are used for counting the recitation of the "Hail Mary" prayer. Each set is then separated by another single, usually larger, bead, signaling the repeating of the "Our Father," or Lord's Prayer. The prayer beads used by Buddhists, Hindus, and Muslims are also sometimes called rosaries.

Brown used to keep the entire rosary collection, along with religious statues and old coins, in a room at his modest home in North Bonneville, Washington, and was always gracious about showing visitors around. As he grew older and the collection expanded, major museums contacted Brown asking him to sell or give them his collection. But Brown wanted to keep the collection close to home, so he arranged to have all 4,000 rosaries put on permanent display in a special room at the Skamania County Museum in Stevenson, Washington.

There are rosaries here made from bone, semiprecious stones, olive pits, nuts, deer antlers, plastic pop-beads, and even one made from ping-pong balls by a nun from Alaska (perhaps so she could count her prayers with her mittens on?). All sizes are represented, from tiny rosaries stored inside acorns to the largest rosary in the world—16 feet, 3 inches—made of spray-painted Styrofoam balls for a school play in Massachusetts. There's a rosary made from lead bullets, a glow-in-the-dark rosary, and one designed to be attached to an automobile steering wheel so the driver can pray on the road. There's even an American flag made out of 39 rosaries. Rosaries from famous people—such as Lawrence Welk, John F. Kennedy, Robert Kennedy, and Al Smith, who in 1928 was the first Catholic to run for president of the United States—are also here.

The rosaries are strung across curtain rods and on birdcage hangers inside eight floor-to-ceiling glass cases. When Brown was alive he insisted that the cases remain open so people could touch the rosaries and rub their own beads against the museum's to transfer the blessing. Surprisingly, some people actually stole the rosaries—one has been pilfered (and recovered) three times. Now the museum cases remain locked.

The collection is still growing. In the same way that Don Brown accepted rosaries sent to him from around the world, the Skamania County Historical Museum maintains the rosary collection as a "living exhibit" and continues to add donated rosaries to the collection.

NOTE: If fund-raising efforts are successful, there are plans to move the museum to the Columbia Gorge Interpretive Center, so call ahead.

Skamania County Historical Museum • PO Box 396, Stevenson, Washington 98648 • (509) 427-5141 extension 235.
Admission: Free. Hours: Mon–Sat 12pm–5pm, Sun 1pm–6pm. To get there: Highway 14 turns into 2nd Avenue in Stevenson. Turn north on Russell at the flashing yellow light. Turn right at the stop sign onto Vancouver Avenue. The museum is located in the basement of the Courthouse Annex, on Vancouver Avenue.

A Fine Sense of Style

TACOMA
Sara Little Center for Design Research, Tacoma Art Museum

An unmarked door in the Tacoma Art Museum is the gateway to a shrine to design. The Sara Little Center for Design Research, named for its distinguished creator, is devoted to the basic elements of design at all levels. Curator Mary Clure likes visitors to look at designs from all over the world, make connections between them, and ask, "How do they affect my life? What can I learn from them?"

Sara Little, a highly successful product design consultant whose client list included Corning, Neiman-Marcus, Revlon, General Mills, and 3M (she now teaches creative problem-solving in the graduate business school at Stanford University), had a concise design philosophy. She has written: "The point of good design is to humanize. I firmly believe designers should spend more time sensitizing themselves, giving themselves the thrill of seeing relationships between epochs, betweens nationalities, between end uses."

Little moved to Tacoma in 1971. She had long been interested in developing a resource for design students, and she offered the Tacoma Art Museum materials and expertise for the project. The result is the Design Center. The elegant L-shaped room that houses it was modeled on Little's own New York City apartment. It makes use of classic Japanese design principles: economy of space, simplicity, a combination of functionality and beauty.

The room may seem sparse, but behind the closet doors and sliding drawers that cover nearly every wall is a wealth of material—some 5,000 pieces altogether. The objects, which seem eclectic and randomly chosen at first—a woven snowsuit from northern Japan, Thai woven hats, a row of cookbooks, some

From ceramic boxes to fishing vests, Sara Little's designs are full of neat surprises.

African statues, a few photos under glass on a small coffee table—have been chosen as carefully as the paper and ink for a Japanese sketch, and are grouped to inspire leaps of creative thought. Opening a closet to display an exquisite set of stacking ceramic boxes, Clure says, "Yes, these are lovely little things, but wouldn't that shape also be a good design for a condominium complex?" A set of nesting red lacquered trays from Japan is reflected in dinnerware designed by Little for Corning. Pointing out a series of chocolate molds hanging on a wall next to a shelf of cookbooks, Clure says, "The idea is that if you're designing something like molds to make chocolate, you should learn everything about how chocolate is made so that you'll have a close connection with the product."

Another major element concerns body decoration—everything from tattoos to saris. One closet holds several outfits Little used when traveling in the forties and fifties as a design consultant, and addresses several design problems. Problem: How do you travel around the world without taking 14 suitcases? Answer: Commission an elegant, practical, and comfortable gray wool suit from Chanel; under it wear silk blouses with no sleeves and snap-in, easily changed fake cuffs. And for the feet, a single pair of clear Lucite pumps that let brightly patterned stockings show through. Problem: How to travel in Africa and stay as mobile as possible? Answer: Appropriate and adapt your husband's multipocketed fishing vest and become your own luggage. Problem: How to give a lecture at a seminar and (despite being under 5 feet tall) make a statement and stand out? Answer: Wear a boldly colored Givenchy silk jacket.

Work-study students and museum staff act as docents to show visitors through the collection. Take advantage of them when you go; each of Little's objects is beautiful in itself, but the collection's purpose as a whole will remain tantalizingly abstract without expert guidance.

Tacoma Art Museum • 1123 Pacific Avenue, Tacoma, Washington 98402 • (206) 272-4258

Admission: $3 for adults, discounts for children and senior citizens; free on Tues.
Hours: Tues–Sat 10am–5pm, Thurs 10am–7pm, Sun 12pm–5pm. **To get there:**
From I-5 take exit 133 and follow the City Center signs; the museum is downtown,
on the corner of 12th Street and Pacific Avenue.

One of the 60,000 outstanding
Asahel Curtis photographs owned by
the Washington Historical Society.

Junk Mail from Long Ago

TACOMA
Washington Historical Society Museum

In a beautiful Victorian building overlooking Commencement
Bay, the Washington Historical Society preserves and displays
over 100 years' worth of anthropological artifacts from the state,
concentrating on the legacies of people, as opposed to the legacy
of the land. The holdings include some 35,000 three-dimensional
pieces, 4 million photos (including 60,000 by Asahel Curtis
alone), over one million documents, several thousand maps, an
extensive postcard collection begun at the turn of the century, and
about 1,500 Native American woven baskets. This last collection

inspired Tacoma native and glass artist Dale Chihuly to begin his famous "basket" series of glassworks.

The Society recently reopened its handsome public exhibition hall after extensive remodeling, and one highlight of the permanent exhibit is the original covered wooden wagon (complete with original graffiti) that pioneer Ezra Meeker built in 1906, at the age of 76, to commemorate the Oregon Trail. Pulling the wagon (a grizzled mannequin stands in for old Ezra) are, preserved, the oxen that actually took the wagon all the way to Washington, D.C.

Another part of the exhibit features memorabilia from Washington's labor movement. A historically important group of paintings by Ronald Debs Ginther, a cook and self-trained artist active in the local union movement earlier in this century, are rough and almost cartoonish, but they vividly show life on the Seattle picket line or in a waterfront Hooverville. Other labor-related artifacts include a book called *Was It Murder?*, about the Armistice Day massacre in Centralia in 1919, involving the International Workers of the World, or Wobblies, and *The Desert of Wheat*, an anti-Wobbly novel by Western writer Zane Grey published in the same year.

Several thousand examples of handbills, advertisements, and other ephemera, each stored in acid-free archival paper and clear Mylar sleeves, give us a glimpse of daily life in days past. There are items from relatively recent history (a flier emblazoned "Women's March Against The War—Nixon's Secret Plan") and turn-of-the-century handbills. One advertisement touts a wrestler called "the Terrible Turk" and advertises "$1,000 to any man who succeeds in throwing him in one fall." An 1885 brochure about the Northwest, printed in Sweden to attract immigrants, refers to the beauties of "Puget Sund—Landet." (Some immigrant-attracting schemes didn't work too well: one advertises "Chicago, the Garden City of the Sound," which was to be located near Anacortes but never materialized. "There are NO MUD FLATS in Chicago," it reads, "and no Hills to climb.") One flier, neatly labeled "July, 1903," extols the virtues of Miss Virginia, "the Greatest Living Exponent of Occult Science and Palmistry"; a 1910 poster asks, "Who Gave Men the Right to Vote and When?" And a poster advertising the sailing "on or about May 10, 1900" of the "large and magnificent steamship Centennial" takes us back to the rough-and-tumble era of the Cape Nome Gold Rush.

Washington Historical Society Museum • 315 N Stadium Way, Tacoma, Washington 98403 • (206) 593-2830
Admission: $2 for adults, discounts for children and senior citizens. **Hours:** Tues–Sat 10am–5pm, Sun 1pm–5pm. **To get there:** From I-5 take exit 133 to Highway 707. Take a right on Stadium Way to N 1st and Tacoma Avenue. Go right for two blocks, turn right on N 3rd and go downhill two blocks.

A Museum of the Heart

TOPPENISH
Yakima Nation Museum

The Yakima Nation Museum is a museum of the heart, not the head; it educates by evoking emotions and provoking visceral responses. What is on display is less interesting, in many ways, than how it is displayed.

The core of the collection consists of 10,000 books and artifacts—the legacy of Nipo Strongheart, who grew up in nearby White Swan as the grandson of an important Yakima leader. Strongheart became a horseback rider in Buffalo Bill's Wild West Show and, beginning in 1905, a film actor with a 40-year Hollywood career. He willed his collection of Native American artifacts to the Yakima Nation upon his death in 1966.

From outside, the two-story, slightly conical, modern museum building looks a bit like a traditional tule-mat house. Inside, it's cool and quiet and contemplative. Instead of descriptive text on the walls, there are poems. A life-size diorama of a man teaching his son to fish is accompanied by the soothing sounds of water from the falls. The sections between displays are filled with trees, flowers, and bird sounds. A display about the time-ball—the traditional length of knotted and beaded hemp used to recall stories from the past—doesn't give much factual information, but it does give a sense of the role the time-ball filled in daily life.

The intent here is to give visitors a dramatic taste of the life of the Yakimas before the advent of white settlement. White people appear in the exhibits only toward the end of the journey through the museum, with a sobering series of panels telling how the Yakimas, in 1855, were forced onto a reservation that was one-tenth the size of their original lands, and how Indians did not become United States citizens until 1924.

Yakima Nation Museum and Cultural Center • PO Box 151, Toppenish, Washington 98948 • (509) 865-2800
Admission: $2 for adults, discounts for children and senior citizens. Hours: Mar–Dec: Mon–Fri 8am–5pm, Sat 9am–5pm, Sun 10am–5pm. To get there: The museum is just off the intersection of Highway 97 and Fort Road, and is clearly visible from the highway.

A Real 'Gunsmoke' Fan

VANCOUVER
Dodge City

It's hard to miss Dodge City. Just look for the house that's been spray-painted red, green, yellow, white, and blue, with stars of all sizes on the roof. Park and go around the concrete block fence to the side, where a short white gate invites visitors to step into "Ace" Parsons's backyard wonderland.

Ace's wife, Claire, remembers their watching "Gunsmoke" on television together, and when it went off the air they were so disappointed that Ace decided to re-create Dodge City in miniature in the backyard. Some might say the project has gotten a little out of hand: the Parsonses' backyard is more than a Western town, it's a whole gosh-darn Western county, complete with a tiny cemetery, a church with a small cowboy hanging from a tree, plastic cowboys on plastic horses, yellow coyotes on the rocks just outside of town, a train depot, a wagon train on its way into town—and, nearby, Canyon City, Fort Apache, and more!

To make room for his creation, Ace pulled up all the grass in the backyard and replaced it with gravel. He spray-paints it green and blue, to represent land and meandering river, about once a year. Not content with Dodge City, Ace has also reserved a section of the backyard for a frog shrine, where several hundred plastic and plaster frogs can be seen doing several hundred things.

As you might imagine, the inside of the Parsons home is just as colorful as the outside. Claire says that just about the time Ace retired she found him spray-painting in the bathroom—and he just kept going from there. "He's got to do something," she says.

Dodge City • 805 W 15th Street, Vancouver, Washington 98660
Admission: Free. **Hours:** Daylight. **To get there:** Take the Mill Plain exit off I-5. Head west on Mill Plain, which turns into 15th. The house is at the corner of Harney and West 15th streets.

Natural Art

VANTAGE
Ginkgo Petrified Forest Museum

You'll encounter a surprising example of petrified wood before you enter the museum in Ginkgo Petrified Forest State Park. Try not to stub your toe on that large log lying just outside the entrance. It wasn't just toppled—it's a fossilized tree, millions of years old. Step inside and learn how petrified wood like this gets formed. Then set out on a three-quarter-mile hike along the "Trees of Stone" Interpretive Trail.

Can you see Jimmy Durante
in this piece of petrified
ginkgo wood? (We can't.)

In the museum a 12-minute slide show explains the petrifi-
cation process. As we understand it, 15 million to 20 million years
ago this area was mostly lakes and swamps. Logs and limbs that
fell into the lakes or were brought to the area by rivers were
buried and sealed by lava, which kept oxygen out and halted the
natural decomposition of the wood. Over thousands of years the
mineral compounds from the lava penetrated the organic material of the wood and replaced the wood's cell structure, leaving the
originals perfectly preserved as fossilized "trees of stone." Much
later, Ice Age floods, natural erosion, wind, rain, and excavation
(by humans) removed enough material to uncover the petrified
trees.

Included in the museum and in the forest are walnut, spruce,
and Douglas fir trees, and the rarest form of fossilized wood,
ginkgo, a tree that became extinct on this continent but was later
reintroduced from a species that survived in Asia. The museum exhibits "raw" petrified samples that look exactly like sections of living trees, and nearly 200 slices of the lovely polished variety. Look
closely at the examples of "picture wood," slices of fossilized wood
that seem to contain Mother Nature's drawings. We spotted some

lovely landscapes, a formal portrait of a young girl, some ducks floating on a pond, Jimmy Durante, a baboon, and Dagwood Bumstead.

Ginkgo Petrified Forest Museum • Ginkgo Petrified Forest State Park, Vantage, Washington 98950 • Washington State Park information: (509) 856-2700 or (800) 562-0990 (in Washington).
Admission: Free. Hours: Call for hours. To get there: The museum is located in the park interpretive center. The park is located at Vantage, Washington, where I-90 crosses the Columbia River.

Glow-in-the-Dark Rocks

WATERVILLE
Douglas County Historical Museum

The town of Waterville, established in the late 1880s, served first as a stopover for miners and homesteaders and later as the center of a wheat-farming community. Today Waterville's entire downtown is a historic district.

Before you enter the museum, stop to look at the tram car on the front lawn. This is one of two buckets left over from the ambitious Columbia River Tramway, built in 1902 to help move wheat from the plateau west of Waterville to the Columbia River. The tram operated until 1910, sending large bread-pan–shaped buckets filled with wheat down to steamboats on the Columbia River and hauling them back up filled with lumber, supplies, and the infrequent, brave passenger.

The museum was built in 1959 as a gift to the county by Mr. and Mrs. William Schluenz, a generous couple who needed someplace to house their extensive collection of rocks, fossils, and Native American artifacts. All 4,500 pieces of the Schluenz legacy are here, along with Mr. Schluenz's original handwritten collector's diary.

Be sure to ask curator Helen Grande to turn off the lights in the rock room so you can see the glow-in-the-dark specimens. Some of the rocks here are literally from out of this world, especially the 1917 Waterville meteorite. A farmer found the strange rock in his field when it broke an important part on his harvester. He brought the rock with him when he went into town to get a replacement part, and, in a hurry to finish his harvesting, agreed to leave the rock at the hardware store for townspeople to look at. There it stayed for four years, during which time people were "allowed to test their hammering ability" on it. Later the farmer used the meteorite as a decoration in his flower garden before loaning it to a Tacoma museum, which later claimed ownership. Legal battles ensued, and in 1963 the meteorite was finally placed on permanent display in the Douglas County Historical Museum. Helen Grande now guards it. She points out that the meteorite originally weighed in at 82 pounds—but pieces kept getting sliced off it in Tacoma, and now it weighs only 73¼ pounds.

Rocks and meteorites are just part of the museum's holdings. Among the family heirlooms of local residents is a church made out of 3,500 Popsicle sticks (with eight pews inside), a brochure titled "EATS" from the November 1911 Waterville Potato Carnival, and a pair of boots made to order and given to Vitus Fitzgerald by his uncle when Vitus was 13 years old, in 1902. Downstairs there's a nicely labeled display of 30 examples of antique barbed wire, a collection of old typewriters, and a stuffed and preserved two-headed calf standing on top of a water heater.

Douglas County Historical Museum • PO Box 63, Waterville, Washington 98858 • (509) 745-8435
Admission: By donation. Hours: Memorial Day–Oct 15: Wed–Sun 11am–5pm; other times by appointment. To get there: The museum is at the corner of Highway 2 and Chelan Street, next to Pioneer Park.

Apples and Miniatures

North Central Washington Museum

Wenatchee is known as the "Apple Capital," and the history of the apple industry is well-documented in the North Central Washington Museum. Most ap-peeling is the wallful of colorful apple box labels with evocative names: A-Plus, Bo-Peep, Peter Pan, Buckaroo, Twin Peaks, and of course, William Tell and Yum Yum. The museum's "apple annex" room includes apple-sorting equipment, which is sometimes demonstrated for visitors, but unfortunately we didn't get to see the apple catapult in action.

Upstairs, there's a real treat for railroad buffs—a large coin-operated railroad that's a model of the old Great Northern Railway route over the Cascades. The train travels through turn-of-the-century switchbacks, tunnels, and two bridges in approximately the same spot along the route where they used to be. Among the items in the museum's original wooden exhibit cases we spied a "Bed Bug Poison Dust Bellows," which was used for "blowing poison into corners where bugs hid out during daytime." Downstairs there's a sweet Victorian house built right into the museum's front hall. It was a class project of the Wenatchee Valley College Building Technology program, and the students no doubt all got A's for the beautiful bedroom, parlor, kitchen, and front porch they constructed.

Easily the most unusual exhibit in this museum is the exotic selection of items from the Charbneau-Warren Miniature Collection. The pieces here were once part of a much larger, world-famous collection of miniatures begun in 1900 by a 16-year-old apprentice seaman, Jules Louis Charbneau. His collection grew to 30,000 pieces and was exhibited at the 1939–1940 San Francisco Golden Gate International Exhibition and elsewhere around the world.

Isabella Charbneau Warren, Charbneau's daughter and a longtime Wenatchee resident, inherited the collection and gave 94 items to the museum. Our favorites were the world's smallest bell, the six hand-crocheted bean-size hats, and the elaborate scenes painted on a pinhead, a grain of rice, and a pea. The display of 11 types of knots tied by a Boy Scout, each no larger than a quarter-inch, is also a winner.

NOTE: If you still hunger for more information about apples, stop at the Washington Apple Commission Visitor Center (at the intersection of Alt 97 and Route 2). Although this is clearly a promotional center sponsored by the apple industry, it's refreshing to sit a moment in this air-conditioned spot; you can watch a short film about apples and apple picking, sample cool apple juice, and taste local apples and apple products.

North Central Washington Museum • 127 S Mission Street, Wenatchee, Washington 98807 • (509) 664-5989
Admission: By donation. **Hours:** Mon–Fri 10am–4pm, Sat–Sun 1pm–4pm. **To get there:** The museum is near downtown Wenatchee at the intersection of Mission and Yakima streets.

Mamie Thompson's Stove

WILBUR
Big Bend Historical Society
Museum

The town of Wilbur is named after early settler Samuel Wilbur Condon, a man who later became known as "Wild Goose Bill" because he shot a gaggle of what he swore were wild geese. Those geese turned out to have been the prized pets of a local priest. Condon's ability to assess a situation apparently never improved much. In 1895 he went to a nearby ranch to try to persuade Millie Dunn to return to him. When she resisted, Condon shot and wounded her. Condon then lost a gunfight with the man who came to Millie's rescue. Today Condon's gun, "taken from his hand following his death" in that shootout, rests in the Wilbur museum's "founding father" display.

The museum also boasts a set of souvenir plates from all 50 states, a "radio room" with radios dating back to the early 1920s, two 50-foot shelves of bottles and decanters, and Mamie Thompson's old stove, the first electric stove in the area.

Other museum highlights include the women's jail cell from the original Lincoln County Jail and a display dedicated to the area's most famous outlaw and murderer, Harry Tracy, who in 1902 shot himself in the eye rather than be captured. A larger Tracy exhibit is at the Lincoln County Museum down the road in Davenport.

Big Bend Historical Society Museum • Cole Street, Wilbur, Washington 99185 • (509) 647-5772 or (509) 647-2218
Admission: Free. Hours: June–Aug: Sat 2pm–4pm; other times by appointment. To get there: Traveling east on Route 2, turn left on Raymond Street at Sandy's grocery store and another left on Cole Street. The museum is in an old church building on your right.

License Plates and Ice Scrapers

WINTHROP
Methow River KOA Campground

Mike Meyers is the consummate collector, a man after our own hoarding hearts. He's got 35,000 license plates and 500 ice scrapers—the largest such collection, he believes, in the world. He hasn't quite figured out a way to display the ice scrapers, but he does display several hundred license plates at the KOA campground in Winthrop, and several hundred more at 3-Finger Jacks, on Bridge Street, across from the Information Center downtown.

Meyers started his license-plate collection as a young boy, when his father gave him his old plates every time he bought a new car. One day a friend of his father's who worked at the Department of Motor Vehicles showed up with several hundred

retired license plates in a box. Now Meyers has plates from all over the world, including many from the republics of the former Soviet Union, some that belonged to members of Congress and foreign diplomats, and an unclaimed vanity plate made for Fawn Hall.

Some of Meyers's favorite—and rarest—license plates come from the early days of the automobile, when some states made steel license plates covered with enameled porcelain. The porcelain chipped, but it never faded or rusted, and the colors are as bright as the day they were made.

If you do stop by the license-plate display, ask if Mike is in town. You may get an invitation to see his ice-scraper collection, or maybe his radiator emblems, antique casino chips, armadillos, or airline souvenirs.

Methow River KOA Campground • PO Box 305, Winthrop, Washington 98862 • (509) 996-2258
Admission: Free. **Hours:** Call for hours. **To get there:** The campground is east of Winthrop on Highway 20.

The Pistol in the Tree

WINTHROP
Shafer Historical Museum

While most of Winthrop's downtown storefronts sport imitation early-1900s faded wood, it's up the hill at the Shafer Historical Museum where you'll get a real feeling for the lifestyle of the area's pioneer families.

The centerpiece of the museum complex is a finely crafted log house that once belonged to Guy Waring, an early settler who opened Winthrop's first general store and later owned almost every building on the town's main street. Waring built the house, which became known locally as "The Castle," to entice his wife to move West with him from Boston. The cabin looks cozy enough, with several organs, fine living-room furniture, and even a bear rug on the floor in front of the fireplace.

The rest of the complex replicates an early Methow Valley settlement, complete with a homesteader's cabin, an assayer's office, a barn housing a buggy and stagecoach, a millinery shop, a fire engine (a wagon with a large water barrel on top), a print shop, and a general store. The telephone switchboard used at the Twisp exchange, the original door hinges from an early Winthrop building, and Winthrop's turn-of-the-century post office window are kept safe in the museum, along with "a horse hide coat worn by Allen Davis on stagecoach from Pateros to Winthrop."

In the general store there's a piece of a tree that has grown around an old pistol. The story that accompanies this framed artifact claims that at the foot of the tree a prospector found a pile of bones from a man and a bear. The pistol was apparently thrown out of the man's hand in a "furious fight" and the limbs of the tree grew around the pistol.

If you visit Winthrop in the summer, watch for the weekend Ice Cream Sundae Socials.

Shafer Historical Museum • PO Box 46, Winthrop, Washington 98862 • (509) 996-2712

Admission: By donation. **Hours:** Opens '49er's Weekend, the second weekend in May; June–Aug: every day 10am–5pm. **To get there:** The museum is above Winthrop's main street, Riverside Drive. There's a path up the hill that starts just over the covered wooden bridge toward the south end of Riverside. Or, you can head up Bridge Street to Castle Street, turn right, and continue a few blocks until you see the museum complex on your right.

A Man of the Hills

YAKIMA
Yakima Valley Museum

There are three collections of note in the handsome Yakima Valley Museum. One is a varied group of horse-drawn vehicles. Another concerns the apple, the most celebrated crop of the Yakima Valley. The third is a memorial to Supreme Court Justice William O. Douglas, Yakima's most famous son.

The 50 mint-condition horse-drawn carriages on display were collected by Louis Gannon and his son William, who lived in Mabton, a small town south of Sunnyside. A landau, circa 1890, is described as "the closest carriage to a vehicle of state in the United States. . . . Every livery stable tried to have one for hire, for visiting dignitaries. . . ." The sign on the 1900 surrey (which, yes, has a fringe on top) points out that this type of vehicle was suitable for families (as opposed to a buggy, which held only two passengers). A wicker phaeton, circa 1905, was designed to carry only one passenger—in this case, a woman, to judge by its dainty parasol.

Some 60 different fruit, vegetable, grain, seed, forage, and specialty crops are grown in the Yakima Valley; Yakima County is ranked fifth overall in agriculture out of 3,072 counties in the United States, and is number one in apple, mint, and hops production. Its most celebrated crop is the apple, and the Yakima Valley Museum has a number of apple-related items, including a 1905 horse-drawn orchard sprayer and a vintage apple brusher (which looks like a giant coin-op shoe brusher). Best of all are several walls' worth of colorful vintage apple-box labels and ads, including labels for Yum-Yum, Repetition, Chief Seattle (in which the chief appears to be wearing an Elizabethan leather jerkin), and Appletizin ("Johnny Appletizin says: They're Full-O-Health"). Over 5,000 more original labels are in the museum's archives and can be inspected by appointment. Some are also available for purchase in the gift shop.

William O. Douglas was valedictorian of the Yakima High School class of 1916 and later graduated from Whitman College in Walla Walla and Columbia Law School. In 1936 he was appointed to the Securities and Exchange Commission, and the following year he became its chairman. He was involved in a massive reorganization of Depression-era Wall Street, and appointed to the U.S. Supreme Court in 1939.

William O. Douglas, flanked by Senator Warren G. Magnuson (left) and Edward R. Murrow (far right), examines an exhibit at the centennial celebration for the Washington Territory in 1953.

Douglas set two records as an associate justice, for longevity on the bench (36 years) and for number of decisions written (over 1,200). He was a fiery champion of First Amendment rights, individual liberty, and environmentalism—stands that did not always endear him to everyone, least of all many Yakima residents who knew him way back when. Douglas was also a distinguished author, outdoorsman, and traveler; his love for the wilderness—especially the mountains near Yakima—prompted him to write several books on the subject. Douglas retired from the bench in 1975 and died five years later. When ordering flags to fly at half-staff in Douglas's honor, then-President Jimmy Carter called him "a lionlike defender of individual liberty." Justice Brennan called him "the only true genius I have ever known."

The Douglas estate bequeathed a large collection of memorabilia to the Yakima Valley Museum shortly after Douglas's death. Much of it still awaits processing, including his publications, thousands of photos and slides from his travels, extensive correspondence, and the original manuscripts of hundreds of speeches. But a good portion of the Douglas Collection is already on display. There is a nearly exact replica of his Supreme Court chambers, and a lunchbox emblazoned with the stenciled words "Douglas For President," dating from a short-lived 1952 grassroots campaign to draft him for that office. The exhibit also displays the official proclamation making him a member of the Court, his judicial robes, and his imposing leather Court chair.

Yakima Valley Museum • 2105 Tieton Drive, Yakima, Washington 98902 • (509) 248-0747
Admission: $2.50 for adults, discounts for children and senior citizens. **Hours:** Tues–Fri 10am–5pm, Sat–Sun 12pm–5pm. **To get there:** The museum is in Franklin Park, west of downtown. Take Yakima Avenue west to 16th Avenue and turn left. Go approximately four blocks to Tieton Drive and turn right. Go three blocks and look for the parking lot.

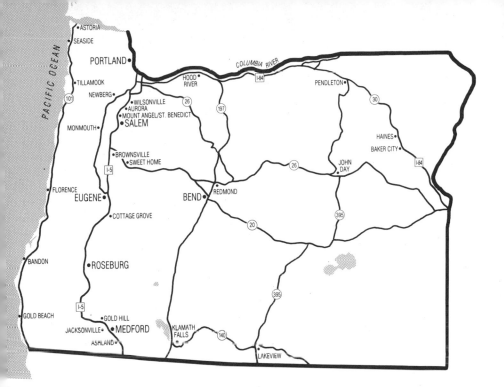

Oregon

Jeanne Daugherty as Viola and George Smith as Malvolio in *Twelfth Night*, from the Oregon Shakespeare Festival's first season, in 1935.

Once More unto the Breach

Oregon Shakespeare Festival Exhibit Center

In 1935 Angus Bowmer, an English professor at Southern Oregon Normal School (later Southern Oregon State College), persuaded the town of Ashland to let him build a makeshift stage on the site of the old Chautauqua dome. He used the new facility to launch an event that was to become a mainstay in the lives of Pacific Northwest theater lovers—the Oregon Shakespeare Festival. Bowmer's first productions, *The Merchant of Venice* and *Twelfth Night*, were mounted that season, along with boxing matches, which were held to defray costs. (Instead, the boxing lost money and had to be bailed out by the success of the theatrical venture.) Now the Ashland festival presents as many as 12 new productions annually in three theaters. Recent seasons have included some 700 performances and a total attendance of over 300,000 yearly.

For Shakespeare fans, and especially for dyed-in-the-wool Ashland regulars, the Festival Exhibit Center—a spacious building housing a collection of Shakespearean memorabilia—is a must. Mannequins sport costumes and props from the previous year's productions next to exhibits of vintage photos and playbills. A short film details the technical intricacies of making quick set changes during a typical day at the festival's three theaters. Photographs honor festival actors—among them Kyle MacLachlan, William Hurt, George Peppard, and Stacy Keach—who have gone on to wider fame.

Best of all, you can be Hamlet, King Lear, or Juliet for a little while yourself. Upstairs in the Exhibit Center is a room where you can try on a variety of costumes and hats, then pose before backdrops while holding an appropriate (or inappropriate, if you'd rather) prop. Be sure to bring your camera—there's nothing like a snapshot of yourself in a dashing Florentine hat or a high-waisted Elizabethan gown for a laugh when you get home.

NOTE: The Exhibit Center is included in the festival's backstage tour, although it can also be visited on its own. Children under 5 cannot take the backstage tour, for safety reasons, but are welcome at the Exhibit Center. Visitors can sign up for a tour of backstage or of the museum, even if not attending plays.

Oregon Shakespeare Festival Exhibit Center • 15 S Pioneer Street, PO Box 158, Ashland, Oregon 97520 • (503) 482-4331
Admission: $2 for adults, discounts for children. Hours: Feb–Oct: Tues–Sun 10:30am–1:30am. To get there: Take I-5 to Ashland and follow the signs to the Center.

Backstage tour: (503) 482-4331
Admission: $7.50 for adults, discounts for children. Hours: Feb–Oct: Tues–Sun; the tour begins at 10am at the Black Swan, and lasts about two hours.

Early Days of Sail

ASTORIA
Columbia River Maritime
Museum

The year 1992 marked the 200th anniversary of Captain Robert Gray's discovery of the entrance to the Columbia River. In 1792 the American naval officer became the first non-native to sail up the river; he named it after his ship, *Columbia*. The Columbia River Maritime Museum opened its doors on the 190th anniversary of Gray's discovery, in 1982, in a huge, gray waterfront building that reminds some visitors of a boat and others of a cresting wave.

The Great Hall features restored small craft, and items that trace the maritime industry—from the days of fur trading and exploration to modern fishing, whaling, shipping, and naval activities— are laid out in a sequence of galleries. The first gallery features exhibits on the early exploration of the Columbia River and the Northwest coast. Among the displays is a sampling of goods that white traders and Native Americans used for barter. Hatchets, knives, nails, liquor, and blankets were traded for sea otter and beaver pelts and salmon.

Another gallery focuses on safety and navigational instruments, and displays artifacts from ships that were wrecked at the treacherous entrance to the Columbia River. More than 100 large ships and nearly 2,000 smaller vessels have fallen victim to the raging storms, shifting sand bars, high winds, and huge breakers so common at the mouth of the river, an area that has been dubbed the "Graveyard of the Pacific."

Our favorite items are the artfully arranged exhibit of beacons and buoy lights with red, white, and blue flashing warning lights; the hundreds of colorful salmon labels from the many canneries that once lined the Astoria riverfront; the collection of shiny ships' bells and whistles; and the glass floats of all shapes and sizes that have washed up on Oregon beaches.

Stop by the "Art of the Whaler" exhibit to see what sailors did with their spare time. Whaling voyages sometimes lasted up to five years, so sailors had plenty of time to perfect their embroidery, carving, and engraving skills. An unusual collapsible scrimshaw yarn swift (designed to hold a skein of yarn while the user winds it into a ball) folds up like an umbrella. Other mariner handiwork includes embroidered cushions and capes, cigar-box picture frames, fancy knotwork, and, of course, ships in bottles. The secret of how those many-masted ships fit through the tiny bottlenecks is revealed at the museum, but we're not going to ruin the surprise by telling you here.

Kids enjoy climbing into the replica of a steamboat pilothouse, where they can stand at the helm and turn the 5-foot-high wheel, check the compass, and bark orders to the engine room through the voice tube. Also "climbable" is the navigation bridge from the USS *Knapp*, a destroyer active in the Pacific during the Second World War and the Korean War. When the rest of the ship was dismantled for scrap, the bridge and pilothouse were barged to Astoria, where the museum building was then erected around them.

The lightship *Columbia*, which once served to mark the river entrance, is moored alongside the museum. Visitors are welcome to climb aboard for a self-guided tour.

Columbia River Maritime Museum • 1792 Marine Drive, Astoria, Oregon 97103 • (503) 325-2323
Admission: $4 for adults, discounts for children and senior citizens. **Hours:** Every day 9:30am–5pm; closed Thanksgiving and Christmas. **To get there:** The museum is on the waterfront side of Route 30, at the east end of Astoria.

Sisters of Steel

ASTORIA
Swenson Blacksmith Shop

Karl Swenson ran a bustling blacksmith shop serving Astoria's farmers, loggers, and fishermen for 50 years, until he died in 1967. To honor his memory, his daughters, Leila and Adeline Swenson, keep the shop open as a museum, but they get few visitors because they don't keep regular hours or post a sign out front. This is a "word of mouth" museum, with no heat and no neatly typed descriptive notes. If you want to visit, you need to call ahead, make an appointment, and get directions. If it's winter, the sisters will remind you to be "warmly clothed." Don't be discouraged; it's worth the visit.

As youngsters the Swenson sisters spent all their free time at the shop. Adeline says they'd do their homework, eat their lunch, or just keep warm by the fire "watching the machines rolling and moving." Although they learned what each tool was used for, Leila says Karl never let his daughters help out or touch anything because they were "supposed to be ladies." When their father died, the Swenson sisters were urged to break up the shop, sell all the handmade tools, and clean out the building. But they just couldn't bring themselves to do it. Instead they kept everything exactly the way their father had left it, so they could show visitors how he made the crab rings, boat blades, wagon wheels, knives, and other items needed by Astoria's townspeople. Everything the Swenson sisters pick up they put back in exactly the same spot. That includes the piles of washing machine and lawnmower pieces Karl collected in case he needed an extra part. Karl Swenson's work clothes, coat, Stetson hat, and even his vest remain exactly where he last put them down, more than 25 years ago.

Leila and Adeline Swenson say that they're old enough to be "retired, plus" and that they're only beginning to think about what might happen to the museum in the future. In the meantime they have no plans to put up a sign, print a brochure, or establish permanent hours. As long as they're able, they'll keep the Blacksmith Museum intact and open to visitors who can find it.

Swenson Blacksmith Shop • 1795 Duane Street, Astoria, Oregon 97103 • (503) 325-2203 (Clatsop County Heritage Museum)
Admission: Free. **Hours:** Tues, Thurs, Fri 9am–12pm, depending on the weather.
To get there: Call ahead for directions.

Putting Out Fires

ASTORIA
Uppertown Firefighters Museum

Thomas Byrne (as in burn) vows that he "didn't know the difference between a Greyhound bus and a Ford convertible" when the Clatsop County Historical Society assigned him to staff Astoria's Uppertown Firefighters Museum. Now, after reading every fire-fighting history book he could find and questioning every fire fighter who would talk to him, he realizes "why these old things have magic," and you'll have to wait for the fact-filled Byrne to take a deep breath if you want to squeeze in a question.

Much of Astoria was built, both physically and economically, on timber, so fire was a frequent and much-feared enemy. Astoria's most memorable fire started downtown in the early morning hours of December 8, 1922. It spread quickly through a wooden viaduct below the main street, and although the Astoria Fire Department had recently purchased a secondhand high-performance Stutz pumper, fire fighters couldn't pump water from the river fast enough to save much of downtown. Nevertheless, the pumper stayed in use until 1961, when a broken drive shaft forced its retirement. Now it's featured in the museum, as is nearly every fire truck and hose cart the Astoria Fire Department has ever operated. The department used an item as long as it lasted, and stored truly obsolete items in old firehouses around town. The historical society has gathered these treasures from all the storage nooks, dusted them off, and housed them in the Uppertown Fire Station #2. The result is an extensive collection of fire-fighting memorabilia, much admired by experts for the rarity of its items, especially the 1911 American LaFrance Chemical Wagon, which even its manufacturer tried to obtain from the city decades later in exchange for a new model. Astoria turned them down.

When we visited the museum, the second-floor display area was not quite finished; when it does open, be sure not to go up there alone. We hear there's a firehouse ghost lurking about. He doesn't really bother anyone, but he often makes a lot of noise. We swear we heard him rattling the old wooden fire fighters' lockers as we were leaving the building.

Uppertown Firefighters Museum • 2986 Marine Drive, Astoria, Oregon 97103 • (503) 325-2203 (Clatsop County Historical Society) **Admission:** $4 for adults, discounts for children (includes admission to any two of the three museums sponsored by the Clatsop County Historical Society). **Hours:** Oct–April: Fri–Sun 11am–4pm; May–Sept: Fri Sun 10am–5pm. **To get there:** The museum is on 30th and Marine Drive, on your right-hand side as you enter Astoria on Route 30.

Communal Music

AURORA
Old Aurora Colony Museum

The idea of moving to a commune, sharing all the work, and being part of one big, happy, extended family wasn't simply a 1960s hippie dream. In the nineteenth century, the Shaker, Amana, and Harmony colonies were thriving communal

The Aurora Pioneer Brass Band. Note the "back-thrust" bells on some instruments.

societies in the eastern United States, and Oregon's Aurora Colony was an early and successful communal experiment in the Pacific Northwest.

The Aurora Colony was led by Prussian-born tailor and physician William Keil, a man who turned to preaching when he immigrated to the United States in 1836. His belief that true Christians should share both their labor and their property became popular enough to persuade about 250 followers to travel West with him in the late 1850s in search of land where they could establish a communal settlement. The group wandered around Washington and Oregon before choosing the Oregon spot Keil named Aurora Mills in honor of both his daughter and the sawmill that had occupied the spot.

Aurora's quilts, woven goods, and homemade sausage and ham became widely regarded, and by 1870 the prospering colony owned 18,000 acres of land. Although today the town looks much as it did in the group's heyday, the experiment didn't last very long. Keil's death in 1877, the coming of the railroad, and frontier opportunities that drew younger colony members away from home all eroded Aurora's cooperative spirit. By 1883 the colony had dissolved, and commonly held assets were divided among the remaining society members.

The still-intact town of Aurora became a National Historic District in 1974, and local residents, including descendants of original colony members, keep the historical spirit alive with festivals, quilting events, and tours of the five-building complex now known as the Old Aurora Colony Museum.

Tours include a short, well-made slide show describing the colony's founding, and exhibits on Aurora quilts and textiles, furniture and farm equipment, and other aspects of daily life in the colony. In the main building, take a moment to listen to the music of the Aurora Pioneer Brass Band and to puzzle over their musical instruments. Of the dozen on display, four feature unusual "backthrust" or "backfire" bells, which were common in civilian marching bands during the Civil War era. These bells "aimed" sound to the rear of the player and helped a small band sound much bigger than it was. A tape from a modern-day concert featuring seven of these restored instruments is part of the exhibit.

The most surprising fact we learned on our tour was the real story behind the kids' song "Pop Goes the Weasel." Sitting at a spinning wheel, our tour guide revealed that although most people believe the ditty is about a little furry animal, it actually refers to the sound made by an ingenious counting device mounted on a weasel, or yarn winder, after it has been turned 100 times.

Old Aurora Colony Museum • PO Box 202, Aurora, Oregon 97002 • (503) 678-5754

Admission: $2.50 for adults, discounts for children. **Hours:** Feb–Dec: Wed–Sat 10am–4:30pm, Sun 1pm–4:30pm; June–Aug: also open Tues, 10am–4:30pm; closed Jan. **To get there:** Aurora is near Canby, Oregon, between Salem and Portland on Route 99E. Take the Canby-Hubbard or Aurora exit. The museum is on the corner of 2nd and Liberty streets, just off 99E, which goes through the center of town. Walking-tour maps, restrooms, and tourist information are available at the museum.

Westward Ho

BAKER CITY
National Oregon Trail
Interpretive Center

Many of the museums you'll find in Oregon and Washington tell the story of how early settlers lived, worked, and played in the late nineteenth century. While daily life out West was perilously difficult for many pioneers, it probably seemed quite manageable after the brutal 2,000-mile trip along the Oregon Trail. The Oregon Trail Interpretative Center tells the story of how those courageous settlers got here and what the five-month trip was like. Once you've visited the center, you'll appreciate why pioneer museums value so highly a single china teacup or porcelain doll that survived the journey.

The year 1993 marks the 150th anniversary of the Oregon Trail, the route that more than 300,000 pioneers followed from Missouri to Oregon in the largest voluntary mass migration in human history. The Bureau of Land Management (BLM) chose to locate the interpretive center at Flagstaff Hill near Baker City after surveying sites from Missouri to Oregon that still retained visible evidence of the trail. From scenic overlooks visitors can view 13 miles of the trail route, including wagon wheel ruts that mark the pioneers' path. By the time the settlers reached eastern Oregon, they had "only" 400 miles left to go to reach Oregon's Willamette Valley. The lushness of the Baker Valley and the forested Blue Mountains before them must have seemed inviting.

Both the indoor complex, with its interactive gallery displays, and the outdoor living-history demonstrations are designed to offer visitors an experience of what it felt like to walk and ride along the Oregon Trail in 1843. All the quotes posted near the displays, the scripts for the audiotapes, and the words spoken by volunteers who participate in the outdoor exhibits come directly from the diaries and journals of the early pioneers. Inside there are no barriers between the visitors and the exhibits. You walk alongside a group of settlers headed West—a wagonmaster leading four wagons hitched to mules and oxen, a mother and her daughter gazing wistfully back over the trail, and a young man pushing his belongings in a large wheelbarrow, dreaming of Gold Rush country. Although they're mannequins, your presence in the gallery activates audiotapes that fill the air with the sound of trail chatter, creaking wagon wheels, clinking chains, and bellowing oxen. A young boy of about 7 sits in the back of one of the wagons and holds out a branch to a billy goat. When his tape begins, he's wondering what school will be like out West.

As you wend your way along the trail, across the continent, everything you see looks authentic, and mostly it is. Authenticity was so important to the center staff that they rejected the first oxen sent over by the taxidermist because they belonged to a species bred later than the species that would have pulled the immigrants' wagons. The same thing happened with the first herd of sheep.

As the settlers make their way along the trail, listen to a Native American couple bartering with a white couple outside a buffalo-cowhide tepee. The white woman is offering an apron for a beautiful pair of beaded moccasins. Then, witness a dangerous river crossing and, once the pioneers make it across the river, use the "touch board" at their campsite to choose subjects you'd like to learn more about. Choose "medicine" or "evening activities" and shadows inside the tents will share stories.

When the pioneers arrive at Oregon City, the end of the Oregon Trail, there's a special treat. The video at this exhibit includes original film footage of 87-year-old Ezra Meeker, who traveled the length of the trail west to east in 1906. The film shows Meeker taking the wheels off a covered wagon and paddling it across a river. (For a look at his wagon and the actual [preserved] oxen that pulled it, see the entry on Tacoma's Washington Historical Society Museum, in the Washington section.)

This center is the first of four interpretive centers that will be built to commemorate the history and heritage of the Oregon Trail. The BLM plans to build one east of Pendleton on the Umatilla reservation, another near The Dalles, and the third at the end of the trail, in Oregon City.

National Oregon Trail Interpretive Center • Flagstaff Hill, PO Box 987, Baker City, Oregon 97814 • (503) 523-1843
Admission: Free. Hours: Oct–Apr: every day 9am–4pm; May–Sept: every day 9am–6pm; closed Christmas and New Year's Day. To get there: Flagstaff Hill is located 5 miles east of Baker City. From Interstate 84 take Route 86 east and follow signs.

Rock Hounds

BAKER CITY
Oregon Trail Regional Museum

I n an old natatorium (or indoor swimming palace) in downtown Baker City is the Oregon Trail Regional Museum, home to a large rock and mineral collection described by some as "the best in the West." The bulk of the 15-ton collection of rocks, minerals, fossils, and semiprecious stones belonged to sisters Elizabeth

Cavin Warfel and Mamie Cavin. The pair became rock hounds in the mid-1930s after a classmate in Elizabeth's mineralogy class dropped and broke a rock specimen. Elizabeth scooped it up and the collection began.

The sisters combed the mountains for specimens and, with their own rock-cutting equipment, mastered the art of slicing, cutting, and polishing their finds. In 1960 the women and their rocks moved to California, where the collection continued to grow in both size and notoriety.

When Elizabeth died, Mamie got loads of offers to purchase the collection, but none suited her. She decided instead that the collection should return home to Baker. Several heavy semitrailer-loads later it did, and now visitors can enjoy displays that include geodes, fossils, shells, corals, jewels, and a 1,000-pound Arkansas crystal. And the collection doesn't stop with rocks. The old natatorium has a wide array of covered wagons, buggies, and other pioneer artifacts.

Oregon Trail Regional Museum • 2490 Grove Street, PO Box 214, **Baker City, Oregon 97814** • (503) 523-9308
Admission: $1.50. Hours: Mid-May–mid-Oct: every day 9am–4pm. To get there: The museum is at Campbell and Grove streets, in a large brick building across from the city park.

Joe Namath's Helmet

BANDON
Professional Sports Hall of Fame Museum

Bruce Buseman admits, "I tried to be a pro ball player and I wasn't any good, so I decided the only way I could get into it was by collecting memorabilia." He gathered so many "game-used" jerseys, helmets, caps, bats, balls, and other items that

he's opened a part of his collection to the public in an unofficial but entertaining gallery in the downstairs of his home. It's a must for sports nuts.

Buseman buys and sells, so his collection is always changing. Sports memorabilia is big business these days; when we spoke with him, Buseman was on the verge of selling the jersey that Gary Cooper wore as Lou Gehrig in the movie *Pride of the Yankees*; he'd set the minimum bid at $95,000. A real Gehrig jersey had sold not long before for $365,000.

"You name him, we've got him here," Buseman says. Among the 350-odd jerseys on display (out of a total of 3,200 in Buseman's possession) are ones from such greats as Jim Brown, Magic Johnson, Dizzy Dean, Walter Payton, Ken Griffey, Jr., and Willie Mays. There are also shoes from Terry Porter of the Portland Trail Blazers. Ty Cobb's glove. Ted Williams's shirt. The jersey Nolan Ryan wore when he pitched his fourth shutout. Steve Garvey's World Series jersey. Joe DiMaggio's glove. Joe Namath's helmet. The fight robes of Rocky Marciano and Mike Spinks. "I'm stronger on the older stuff," Buseman explains, "but you've got to have the younger players too, because the kids don't know the old guys."

An entire showcase is devoted to the legendary Bobby Doerr, who played for the Red Sox from 1937 to 1951, was inducted into the Baseball Hall of Fame in 1986, and has been an Oregon resident since the 1940s. Oregon-born Hall of Famer and perennial All-Pro defensive tackle Bob Lilly, who spent his entire career with the Dallas Cowboys, is also featured. There's one non-sports item of note: a gold record autographed by Elvis Presley. Buseman claims he visited Graceland in the early 1970s with his cousin, who had appeared in one of the King's movies, and ended up trading $900 and Norm ("the Flying Dutchman") van Brocklin's Rams shirt for the gold record.

Professional Sports Hall of Fame Museum • Route 1, Box 1312, Bandon, Oregon 97411 • (503) 347-4547
Admission: $2 for adults, discounts for children. **Hours:** June–Sept: Wed–Sun 10am–5pm; other times by appointment. **To get there:** The museum is 8 miles south of Bandon on Highway 101.

Celebrating the Desert

BEND
High Desert Museum

There are live owls, snakes and lizards, a family of otters headed by Bert and Ernie, and porcupines named Thorndyke, Cactus, and Spike—all living happily in natural settings at the High Desert Museum. Laid out like a nature preserve, the museum has 20 acres of outdoor trails with trailside exhibits, presentations, and a re-created turn-of-the-century sawmill. Indoors it houses a major collection of Native American artifacts, and paintings and photographs by such well-known artists as Charles Russell and Edward Curtis.

This constantly expanding museum offers an in-depth taste of the cultural history and natural resources of the high desert, an area that spans eight western states and British Columbia, and includes a delicately balanced mix of timberland, rivers, volcanic hot springs, and—you guessed it—desert.

The combination of live animals and historic displays is designed

Bernie Jestrabek-Hart used barbed wire to sculpt this mare and foal.

to provide a greater understanding of and concern for the region's heritage and preservation. Artifacts are used in realistic settings rather than placed in glass cases. A pioneer cabin is furnished with a handmade quilt, and a pie sits half-finished in the kitchen on a table strewn with the appropriate utensils. In the Hall of Exploration and Settlement visitors feel the warmth from a kettle steaming in a cowboy's bunkhouse, hear the clang of a blacksmith's anvil, and may find themselves looking around for the Northern Paiute Indians who seem to have just stepped away from their camp.

Plan to spend all day here, because there's a lot to see and a lot of ground to cover. And don't rush by the large sculpture of a mare and her foal along the path to the museum's entrance. Boise artist Bernie Jestrabek-Hart made it out of ungalvanized barbed wire, a medium that ranks right up there with cows and cowboys as a potent symbol of how newcomers changed the West.

High Desert Museum • 59800 S Highway 97, Bend, Oregon 97702 • (503) 382-4754
Admission: $5.50 for adults, discounts for children. **Hours:** Every day 9am–5pm; closed Thanksgiving, Christmas, and New Year's Day. **To get there:** The museum is 6 miles south of Bend on Route 97.

Life Out West

Linn County Historical Museum

O odles of historical memorabilia in life-size dioramas portray daily life in the Linn County area at the turn of the century. There's a well stocked general store, a bank, a barbershop, a milliner's shop, a blacksmith shop, and exhibits that depict early manufacturing and agricultural activities. The scene is so realistic that the mannequins in the displays prompted one young visitor to write in the guest book, "I think they're alive. One of them turned and looked at me. Scary."

The exhibits are all housed in Brownsville's former railroad depot, with old Southern Pacific railroad boxcars imaginatively pressed into service as exhibit areas and a minitheater. The covered wagon in the lobby is real, and a rare find. Of the thousands of wagons that came over the Oregon Trail, it's one of only three that remain intact.

Another exhibit that delights visitors of all ages is the wall full of hand-carved, exact-scale models of miniature horse-drawn wagons, carriages, surreys, stagecoaches, and other vehicles of conveyance, all made by Portland resident Willard Austin, a retired electrician. Look for the Wells Fargo stage-coaches, the 20-mule team hauling wagonloads of borax, a milk wagon, a horse-drawn hearse, an Amish covered buggy, and other horse-drawn vehicles that re-create transportation methods dating back to the early 1800s.

Linn County Historical Museum • **101 Park Avenue, PO Box 607, Brownsville, Oregon 97237** • **(503) 466-3390**
Admission: By donation. **Hours:** Mon–Sat 11am–4pm, Sun 1pm–5pm. **To get there:** From Highway 228 take Main Street past Kirk Avenue to Park Avenue. Turn right onto Park. The museum will be on your left.

Biblical Folk Art

BROWNSVILLE
Living Rock Studios

L iving Rock Studios in Brownsville is dedicated to the singular vision of self-taught folk artist Howard Taylor. He was drawn to his three favorite subjects—wildlife, Oregon history, and scripture—because, his daughter Nancy says, "they're what the Lord opened the door for him to do."

Taylor, now in his seventies, collected rocks for years while on the job as a surveyor, and began creating art with rocks nearly 30 years ago when he became disabled and could no longer survey. When he'd made so much art that it needed a separate home, Taylor hand-built the circular Living Rock Studios (Nancy calls it "a mini-castle with a white coolie hat on top") for the public.

The main attraction here is a series of seven huge, translucent, brilliantly colored mosaics depicting Moses and the Burning Bush, the Nativity, and other Bible scenes. Taylor sawed, polished, and glued together hundreds of thin rock pieces to form each scene, then placed them in dark recesses and backlit them for a spectacular effect, not unlike stained glass. Also on display are 100-odd wood carvings, each from a different type of Northwest wood; oil paintings, mostly of local wildlife; and antiques belonging to Taylor's family, which traces its Oregon roots back to the pioneer days around Cottage Grove.

The "Tree of Life" stairway (made of cement and chunks of petrified wood) leads to the second floor, curving past dozens of Taster's Choice coffee jars containing, as Nancy says, "just about every type of rock that a rockhound would want to see"—about 300 altogether. Upstairs is a small amphitheater and a revolving "logging book"—thirty-two 3-foot-high "pages" that hold paintings relating to the early days of Oregon's timber industry.

Taylor and his wife, Faye, are both in poor health now, and Nancy, who lives in nearby Goshen, does her best to keep the studio open on a regular basis. Still, it's a good idea to call ahead and make sure she's around. "If you call ahead," she says, "we can try and have a little extra wood on the fire. It's a little like a cave in here sometimes."

Living Rock Studios • 911 Bishop Way W, Brownsville, Oregon 97327 • (503) 466-5814
Admission: $1. Hours: Tues–Sat 10am–3pm; times vary, so be sure to call ahead. To get there. Brownsville is on Route 228 to Sweet Water (running east from I-5, midway between Corvallis and Eugene). Living Rock Studios is on the right side of the street as you enter Brownsville from the west; look for the petrified tree in the front yard.

Rescued from the Titanic

COTTAGE GROVE
Cottage Grove Museum

As soon as a special cabinet is finished, a maroon woolen overcoat hanging in John and Isabelle Woolcott's hall closet will go on display in the Cottage Grove Museum. Why this particular coat? Because both the coat and its owner (John's mother, Marion Wright) survived the sinking of the *Titanic*!

Until the *Titanic* coat gets its honored spot, sometime in the spring of 1993, museum volunteer John Woolcott says the highlights of the museum will continue to be "an accumulation of

Miners carried this stamp mill into the mountains to separate gold from quartz.

primitive artifacts" used by early pioneers, and memorabilia from early area gold mines, including a model of a water-powered sawmill and a large stamp mill with five 500-pound stamps.

During the area's gold-mining heyday, heavy stamp mills were hauled 4,000 to 5,000 feet up into the mountains and set up wherever water power or a steam engine was available to operate them. Why all the bother? So that miners could separate valuable gold from quartz as quickly as possible. To see how the contraption worked, go inside and switch on the small model and watch how the heavy "stamps" would be lifted up and dropped onto the mined ore, pulverizing and preparing it for a water process that separated the gold from the ore.

The building that houses the Cottage Grove Museum is in itself something of an attraction. Built in 1897 for the Roman Catholic Church, it features Italian stained-glass windows and is supposedly the only octagonal public building in the Pacific Northwest.

Cottage Grove Museum • PO Box 142, Cottage Grove, Oregon 97424 • (503) 942-3963

Admission: Free. **Hours:** June 15–Labor Day: Wed–Sun 1pm–4pm; Labor Day–June 15: Sat–Sun 1pm–4pm. **To get there:** At the corner of "H" and Birch avenues.

Prehistoric Footwear

University of Oregon Museum of Natural History

How old is your oldest pair of shoes? Do you have a pair of negative-heel Earth Shoes or a pair of two-toned saddle shoes you just can't part with?

Whatever you might find in the corners of your shoe closet, you'd be hard-pressed to find foot coverings older than the pair of prehistoric sandals on display at the University of Oregon's Museum of Natural History. The pair here is made out of sagebrush bark and is between 9,000 and 10,000 years old. They were discovered in a cave in eastern Oregon by the museum's first director, Luther Cressman, a man whom collections manager Pamela Endzweig refers to as the "Father of Archaeology in the Pacific Northwest."

In addition to artifacts accumulated in its role as the official repository for state archaeological and anthropological collections, the Oregon Museum of Natural History also has Thomas Condon's valuable and extensive collection of fossils gathered in eastern Oregon during the 1860s. Condon, a preacher who was also Oregon's first geologist, helped prove that many previously unknown prehistoric animals rambled around this region.

The museum maintains an herbarium with plant specimens dating back to 1903 and an important zoological collection, with bird nests and skeletons of birds, fish, and other animals. The collection of bird eggs is especially significant because the eggs were

collected in the 1920s, before pesticides came into use and began
changing the physical structure of shells.

University of Oregon Museum of Natural History • 1680 E 15th Avenue, Eugene, Oregon 97403 • (503) 346-3024
Admission: Free. **Hours:** Wed–Sun 12pm–5pm. **To get there:** From I-5 follow
signs to the University of Oregon campus. The museum is on E 15th Avenue between Agate and Moss streets.

Tying Flies

FLORENCE
Fly Fishing Museum

P rofessional framer William Cushner was minding his own
business in his New York City shop one day in 1969 when
the art director of *Field and Stream* magazine walked in with
some flies he wanted framed. These weren't old houseflies he'd
picked off the flypaper; they were finely handcrafted angler's flies
made by his wife, Helen Shaw, a well-known fly tyer. Cushner had
never heard of fly fishing or fly tyers, but being the imaginative fellow that he was, he set his mind to finding the best way to display
the tiny feathered artworks. Instead of mounting them flat between
a piece of glass and mat, as was the custom, Cushner decided to
attach each fly to a short, thin plexiglass rod. This way the fly would
be slightly suspended in the frame, allowing a better view of the
tyer's handiwork.

Cushner's mounting technique revolutionized the way that
handmade flies were displayed, and Cushner himself was—well,
hooked on the art of fly tying. Although he never went fly fishing
or tied a fly, he did amass a collection of antique flies, some dating back to the 1800s, when the craft of fly tying was popular

among the English aristocracy. Cushner also gathered flies made by contemporary tyers from at least 20 countries around the world. His framed displays paired flies with "angler-inspired" photographs and paintings.

By the 1980s Cushner's fly "inventory" had grown to nearly 50,000 flies and his fly mounting work had become internationally known. His craftmanship was displayed at New York's American Museum of Natural History and at the American Museum of

I ly Fishing in Manchester, Vermont. In 1988 Cushner moved from Nova Scotia to Florence, Oregon, so he could be near family and open his own museum. Although Cushner recently died, his daughter and son-in-law have kept the museum open so that fly tyers and art lovers can continue to enjoy the angling artifacts and handsomely framed flies tied by the world's best.

Fly Fishing Museum • 280 Nopal Street, PO Box 126, Florence, Oregon 97349 • (503) 997-6102
Admission: $2.50 for adults, free for children. Hours: May 15–Sept 30: every day 10am–5pm; other times by appointment. To get there: The museum is in Florence's Old Town section, on Nopal Street. Go one block east of Highway 101 on the "Old Town Loop" on the way to the Port of Siuslaw.

13971. U.S. MAIL BOAT AND PLEASURE PARTY READY TO LEAVE GOLD
THE BEAUTIFUL TRIP UP ROGUE RIVER.   OREGON COAST HIGHWAY

A Roguish Life

Jerry's Rogue River Museum

The Rogue River is one of the wildest and most scenic rivers in the country, with abundant fishing opportunities (it was a favorite of Zane Grey's). At its mouth on the southern Oregon coast, in the little town of Gold Beach, Jerry's Rogue River Museum provides a look at what has formed and inhabited the river—from displays that detail its geological beginnings (the folds and volcanic intrusions that shaped the Oregon coast as a whole) to its wildlife (the museum has mounted examples of native fish and animals, including otter, bear, deer, and a mountain lion). Native American cultures that have lived on the river for at least 8,000 years are represented through artifacts, drawings, and photos. Learn about Lewis and Clark and Jed Smith, and the early days of fishing, logging, and riverboat travel. The museum is a relatively recent addition to Jerry's Rogue River Jetboat Tours, a company that includes among its businesses a gift shop. Owner Bill McNair has operated the company since Jerry's retirement in 1971.

Jerry's Rogue River Museum • Port of Gold Beach, PO Box 1011, Gold Beach, Oregon 97444 • (800) 451-3645 or (503) 247-7601
Admission: Free. Hours: Mon–Sat 9am–6pm, Sun 9am–5pm. To get there: Cross the Rogue River Bridge on the way into Gold Beach and take the first right; Jerry's is right there.

The Northwest's Bermuda Triangle

GOLD HILL
House of Mystery

Between Grants Pass and Ashland, on the banks of Sardine Creek, is a wonderfully hokey roadside attraction that has been puzzling tourists since the 1940s: the House of Mystery, also known as the Oregon Vortex. The story goes that it was created by a man named Lister after he served a little time in

South End – The House of Mystery

prison, where he wrote poetry under an assumed name. He turned this former assayer's shack into an optical-illusion–filled house where "mysterious forces are at work and natural laws are suspended." Water flows uphill, you can stand at a sharp angle to the ground, and your height changes dramatically. Balls tossed over fences bounce back for no apparent reason, brooms stand up by themselves, and normal laws of visual proportion are thrown out of whack.

Is the Vortex a soft spot in the Earth's crust where magnetic forces leak out? Is it true that birds and animals shy away from it? Is that a gleam in the eye of the young person giving you the House of Mystery spiel? We're not telling.

House of Mystery • 4303 Sardine Creek Road, Gold Hill, Oregon 97525 • (503) 855-1543
Admission: $3.50 for adults, discounts for children. **Hours:** June–Aug: every day 9am–4:45pm; Sept–Oct: Fri–Tues 9am–4:45pm; closed Nov–Feb. **To get there:** Take the Gold Hill exit from I-5 and follow the signs.

Pioneer Paraphernalia

HAINES
Eastern Oregon Museum

In 1953 the people of Haines decided that their town needed a large and permanent space in which to exhibit the thousands of pioneer artifacts they wanted to show off (or perhaps to get out of their attics), and a gymnasium built in 1930 was the only space available. Thus was born the Eastern Oregon Museum.

Viola Perkins, a museum volunteer, says it feels "just like Grandma's attic." Others say it looks more like Grandpa's barn.

Well, we doubt that very many grandpas have an entire bar from a Gold Rush saloon packed away in storage, but we'll go along with it.

Everything in the old gym has been pressed into museum service—even the two basketball backboards, which now sport elk heads. The bleachers have been pushed to the center of the gym and placed back-to-back, so that the seats can be used for displaying cooking utensils, crank-style telephones, vintage clothing, carved stone artifacts, and other community-owned collectibles. Along one wall sits the old Bourne Bar, complete with beer kegs and spittoons. Before it was cleaned up for the museum, it was in use as a chicken roost.

Showcases are filled with dishes, clocks, fine lamps, and old newspapers (one details the story of President Lincoln's assassination). Mannequins wear uniforms from several wars. The town's original telephone switchboard is in the museum, too, although Viola Perkins says it hasn't been out of use too long.

Haines's Union Pacific Depot was dragged across the tracks so it could sit beside the museum. It features early railroading items, hand-powered fire-hose carts, and an old fire barrel still filled with water. Among the heavy equipment, which includes an old brewery wagon and several manure spreaders, is a piece of a poplar tree that grew around a well-preserved scythe—probably left there by somebody's grandpa more than 100 years ago, perhaps when Grandma called him in from the fields for dinner, which was served on some of the fine china plates now in the museum.

Eastern Oregon Museum • 3rd and School streets, Haines, Oregon 97833 • (503) 856-3233
Admission: By donation. **Hours:** Apr 15–Oct 15: every day, 9am–5pm; other times by appointment. **To get there:** Haines is between Baker City and North Powder. The museum is four blocks east of US Highway 30, on 3rd Street.

A Fruitful Legacy

Hood River County Historical Museum

Can you name at least four materials that old-time washboards were made of? If not, stop by the washboard display at the Hood River County Historical Museum, where there are boards made of copper, granite, glass, and wood. These and other reminders of the days before automatic washing machines and other timesaving electrical devices are exhibited alongside other household items used by the earliest settlers to the area.

While the Hood River region has recently become a wonderland for another kind of board—the sailboard—the area's history is closely tied to the apple- and pear-growing industries, and both are well documented at the museum. A colorful wall of framed apple-box labels is the background for old fruit-packing tools, including a machine that polished apples before they were boxed and a contraption that made sure box lids were securely fastened.

Inside an early fruit-packing house in Hood River Valley.

The museum's permanent collection includes Native American baskets, stone fishing weights, an odd assortment of old-time musical instruments, and a whiskey still confiscated by the county sheriff's office. Museum coordinator Madeline Edwards has the most fun when locals loan their own collections for display. These special exhibits have run the gamut from an assortment of wedding dresses to a 40-year accumulation of marbles to souvenirs from a stint on the United States Olympic team.

Hood River County Historical Museum • Port Marina Park, Hood River, Oregon 97031 • (503) 386-6772
Admission: Free. Hours: Mid-Apr–Oct 31: Wed–Sat 10am–4pm, Sun 12pm–4pm; other times by appointment. To get there: Take exit 64 off I-84 and follow signs to the Visitor Information Center.

Hands on the Past

JACKSONVILLE
Children's Museum

Many kid-oriented museums focus on science, nature, and various aspects of contemporary life. What makes the Children's Museum in Jacksonville different is its hands-on exhibits that portray the daily life of early Native Americans, pioneers, and settlers from the mid-1800s through 1930. It's one thing to look over a railing at a re-created pioneer cabin; it's quite a different experience to actually try your hand at operating a water pump or a butter churn.

Children's Museum • 206 N 5th Street, Jacksonville, Oregon 97530 • (503) 773-6536
Admission: $1. Hours: Memorial Day–Labor Day: every day, 10am–5pm; after Labor Day: Tues–Sun 10am–5pm. To get there: The museum is at 5th and D streets, in the old jail.

The Last Hanging Rope

JACKSONVILLE
Jacksonville Museum of Southern Oregon History

The entire town of Jacksonville could be considered a living musuem of the late 1800s; its dozens of historic buildings have made the town a popular spot for filming Westerns. Housed in the county's former courthouse, the Jacksonville Museum of Southern Oregon History traces the town's growth from a small gold-mining camp to a bustling trade center to its status as a Historic Landmark City. Look carefully among the exhibits for a short piece of rope. This is someone's "keepsake" from one of the last hangings that took place in the area. Museum staffer Stacey Williams says she doesn't know exactly when that took place, but she does know that it was customary in the area for a hanging rope to be cut up and passed out to townspeople as souvenirs.

Jacksonville Museum of Southern Oregon History • 206 N 5th Street,
Jacksonville, Oregon 97530 • (503) 773-6536
Admission: $1. Hours: Memorial Day–Labor Day: every day 10am–5pm; after La-
bor Day: Tues–Sun 10am–5pm. To get there: The museum is in the old courthouse at 5th and C streets.

Opium and Other Cures

JOHN DAY
Kam Wah Chung & Co. Museum

In the mid-nineteenth century, famine and overpopulation fos-
tered a mass exodus from China. Large numbers of Chinese immigrants made their way to the American West, where there
was high demand for workers in the canning, mining, and railroad
industries. Most of these laborers were single men who hoped to
earn enough money to return to China and start families. Two
who did not were Ing Hay and Lung On, who settled in the tiny
eastern Oregon gold-mining town of John Day in 1887. The
young entrepreneurs set themselves up as shopkeepers, medicinal healers, and all-purpose businessmen, and eventually they became highly respected members of the Chinese community.

"Doc" Hay was known as the most gifted herbal doctor between Seattle and San Francisco. His partner, Lung On, was a
canny businessman and "expediter" who was often called from as
far away as Nevada or Idaho to serve as a mediator in Chi-
nese/Anglo disputes. Their shop, Kam Wah Chung & Co., became
the main center for Chinese life in eastern Oregon. The building
served not only as their home but also as an herbal pharmacy,
mining equipment supplier, general store for Chinese and Western foodstuffs, tobacco shop, legal opium den, gambling house,
Buddhist temple, and (during Prohibition) bootleg whiskey outlet.

The store remained sealed and unused for many years after the deaths of Lung On and Doc Hay in 1940 and 1948, respectively. It was reopened in the 1960s, and since 1977 has been a historical monument, open to the public, that preserves with amazing fidelity the partners' general store, medical offices, and living areas as they once were.

The two-story building is made of stone and wood. It's well-lit now, but you can easily imagine how dark and dismal it was inside, with layers of soot left over from years of opium and incense smoke. Crates of soap and miscellaneous other supplies are still stacked up everywhere. Over 1,000 herbs and other medicinal ingredients are still on the shelves of the medical office, preserved in glass jars and boxes; many are still unidentified, but the identity of some—including such items as beetles, lizard feet, and bat wings—is quite obvious. Sheaves of business correspondence, invoices, letters, and personal papers still lie around. The ornate red-and-gold Buddhist altar and its accompanying religious artifacts are still covered with the smudge of incense. Fruit used as an offering has dried out and become naturally preserved.

Doc Hay's shoes are still underneath his bed; his hats and clothes still hang on the bedroom walls. The bunks where opium smokers lay downstairs are still there, too. Embedded in the kitchen floor is a chopping block for kindling (it was considered bad luck to chop wood outside after dark). The front door and first-floor windows still sport metal shutters used to protect the shop during periodic cowboy raids on "Chinatown."

The guides who show visitors around are full of interesting tidbits of information. One told us that Doc Hay's herbal remedies were often sold sealed in wax balls (the first "tamper proof" bottles); patients bit into the wax to get at the medicine. She told us about the bottles of liquor, nearly 100 in all, that were found hidden behind walls and beneath the building after the partners' deaths. She told us about the $23,000 in uncashed checks found under Doc Hay's bed, and that his bedroom wallpaper came from Sears, circa 1910. It cost 11¢ per roll.

Kam Wah Chung & Co Museum • John Day, Oregon 97845 • (503) 575-0547 (Grant County Chamber of Commerce)
Admission: $2. Hours: May–Oct: Sat–Thurs 1pm–5pm. To get there: The museum is one block off the main street, adjacent to City Park.

Gene Favell with his arrowheads in 1952. Today his collection numbers more than 60,000

60,000 Arrowheads

KLAMATH FALLS
Favell Museum of Western Art and Indian Artifacts

As a kid in Lakeview, Gene Favell was fascinated with natural history, cowboys, the Native American baskets and beadwork his mother collected, and the Indian artifacts he found buried nearby. He started collecting arrowheads when he was 8, and as an adult, when he wasn't running a men's clothing store, he just kept collecting. Every weekend he'd take his six kids artifact hunting around eastern Oregon, and he actively traded Western and Indian memorabilia with other collectors.

By the 1960s his treasure trove had grown so immense—he had roughly 60,000 arrowheads—that he needed a separate building to house it all. The Favell Museum of Western Art and Indian Artifacts, a 17,000-square-foot stone building on the banks of the Link River, opened in 1972. Favell admits it's a "real labor of love—sort of our gift to the community. It's really a fine-arts museum that tells an archaeological story." The museum is an excellent introduction to the history of the West, from ancient times to the rootin'-tootin' days of the frontier, and is the legacy of one man's fascination with those times.

Very young children may be bored—pretty much everything is not to be touched—but older kids who are captivated by cowboys and Indians will have a ball, especially with the two dozen miniature dioramas of frontier life. Favell has been careful to make the place family-friendly, and while some of his museum disregards current politically correct interpretations, he emphasizes that "there's nothing here to antagonize Indians." In fact, there's little here to antagonize anyone; Favell is a quick man with a joke, and various plaques around the museum prove it. For example: "Some paintings are just pigments of an artist's imagination."

Favell's humor may be as corny as Kansas in August, but his museum has some impressive pieces. Included in the collection of Native American artifacts are 1,200 woven baskets, some stunning examples of Anasazi pottery and turquoise jewelry, and an ancient spear-thrower the Aztecs called an *atlatl*. A predecessor to the bow, the *atlatl* and its variations were used all over the world to extend a hunter's throwing arm and give him greater leverage when throwing a spear. Among the Clovis points (a type of heavy spear point used by many Native American tribes) on display here is one made from green glass by the Yahi Indian Ishi (for more Ishi memorabilia, see the entry on Seattle's St. Charles Archery Museum, in the Washington section).

Other standouts include an ancient Nevada tribal cape made of mudhen skins, and stone animal effigies from the banks of the Columbia River. The gem of the museum's 60,000 arrowhead collection is Favell's pride and joy—a brilliantly colored, 1-inch fire opal arrowhead, found in the Nevada desert in 1912 by a sheepherder. The sheepherder sold it for five dollars ("a lot of money in those days") to an Oregon dentist and amateur collector, who tantalized Favell with it for years before finally selling it to him.

By the time Favell seriously began collecting Western paintings and sculpture in the 1960s, well-known artists such as Frederick Remington and Charles Russell were out of his price range. He concentrated instead on contemporary artists, especially those based in Oregon, and represented here are such noted painters and sculptors as John Clymer, Joe Beeler, Harvey Johnson, Ina Pruitt, Don Crook, Frank McCarthy, and Mort Kunstler. (Favell did manage to snag one piece by Russell, a handsome early painting called The Scouts.) One of our favorites in this section, by Kunstler, details the daily life of Paiute Indians, circa 3,000 B.C. In the foreground men are making duck decoys, preparing a fire, and mending fishing nets. A girl carries a woven water bottle on her back, and women are milling seeds and cleaning deer hides. In the background, a couple of hunters are triumphantly carrying an antelope home.

An offshoot of Favell's main interests is his collection of 135 miniature guns ("great for small holdups") displayed in a big walk-in vault. All are in working condition (though in some cases you would need a pencil point to pull the trigger); the exception is a tiny submachine gun, which federal law requires be inoperable. The guns come in a variety of scales, from a 1½-inch-long revolver to an intricate half-size Kentucky long rifle with gold and silver inlays, made by gunsmith Daniel Osterman of Springfield, Oregon. What's next—the Second Amendment inscribed on the head of a pin?

Favell Museum of Western Art and Indian Artifacts • 125 W Main
Street, Klamath Falls, Oregon 97801 • (503) 882-9996
Admission: $4 for adults, discounts for children and seniors. **Hours:** Mon–Sat
9:30am–5:30pm. **To get there:** Follow Main Street from downtown Klamath Falls
across the Link River. The museum is on the other side of the river, on the right-
hand side of the street.

Happiness Is Heirlooms

LAKEVIEW
Schminck Memorial Museum

The Schminck Memorial Museum, like the Whoop N Holler
Museum in Bickleton, Washington, is an example of an
eclectic museum that "just grew" from one family's desire to
preserve their heirlooms, and the surrounding community's desire to help. The museum is housed in a 1922 bungalow that once
belonged to Dalph and Lula Schminck, both descendants of
prominent pioneer families.

The museum was formally established in 1936 after the
Schmincks had spent years collecting just about everything. Curator Charlotte Pendleton says: "They were great packrats, in the pioneer manner; things weren't discarded, but saved and used and
passed down. They were very broad-minded in what they collected, so what's here is a very varied assortment. Both had family members who were always heaping family treasures on
them—he was an only child, and she was youngest. They were
very beloved in the community, and when they declared this place
a museum they said they were forced into it because their friends
kept giving them things and kept pestering them to see things."

The Schmincks died within a few years of each other in the
1960s. The local chapter of the Daughters of the American Rev-
olution took charge and revitalized the collection, expanding it and
establishing a series of formal curators.

Much of the collection, as with other Northwest historical museums, is devoted to furniture and costumes of the Victorian period. But there are also some unusual and specialized items: a barbed-wire collection, several hundred dolls (mostly German bisque), quilts, Indian baskets, saddles, farmyard tools and tack, and a complete collection of *Ladies' Home Journals* from 1897 to 1957. Pendleton's favorite exhibit is the grouping of 150 different patterns of American pressed-glass goblets.

Schminck Memorial Museum • 28 S "E" Street, Lakeview, Oregon 97630 • (503) 947-3134
Admission: $1 for adults, discounts for children. **Hours:** Feb–Nov: Tues–Sat 1pm–5pm; other times by appointment. **To get there:** From Klamath Falls, turn right on Highway 395; the museum is on the east side of the highway, one block south of the junction.

Capturing the Past

MEDFORD
Jackson County History Center

The Southern Oregon Historical Society operates several museums in Jackson County, the site of Oregon's first great gold rush in 1851–1852. The exhibits at the History Center in Medford include "treasures, trinkets, and tidbits," such as 40 horseshoes mounted on a board, and "large amounts" of thimbles, hatpins, and salt and pepper shakers. The remodeled 1940s J. C. Penney Co. department store building also has space for the Historical Society to show off a large collection of antique chairs and old sewing machines, as well as one of those turn-of-the-century bicycles with a giant front wheel. The nineteenth-century photography collection in the research library features 10,000 glass-plate negatives and countless prints made by pioneer

photographer, artist, and horticulturalist Peter Britt, whose work documented the lifestyle and landscapes of southwestern Oregon. His buggy is here too.

Jackson County History Center • **106 N Central Avenue, Medford, Oregon 97501** • **(503) 773-6536**
Admission: Free. **Hours:** Mon–Fri 9am–5pm, Sat 10am–5pm. **To get there:** The museum is located at the intersection of 6th Street and N Central Avenue.

Arctic Treasures

MONMOUTH
Paul Jensen Arctic Museum, Western Oregon State College

P aul Jensen loves to share his experiences, knowledge, and vast Arctic collection with others. And because he's spent 25 of his 85 years living and working with the Eskimo people in Alaska, Canada, and Greenland, he's worth listening to.

Jensen first learned about Eskimo culture in grade school in Denmark, back in 1919. Six Eskimo children were in his class, and his friendship with them sparked his lifetime commitment to studying the Arctic experience. His 4,000-piece collection of artifacts relating to Arctic wildlife and culture is displayed on the campus of Western Oregon State College, where Jensen was a professor of educational psychology until 1979.

Among Jensen's favorite items are an *ulu* (a curved cutting knife) and food trays, which Jensen says amuse visitors because they're almost 4 feet long. Why so big? The large trays are needed to contain the big, messy chunks of whale blubber. "We eat a lot of fatty food in the Arctic, because it gets so cold and windy. You need fat content in your food, such as you get from whale *muktuk*, or blubber." He also favors a simple comb used for harvesting berries. Eskimo grandparents and grandchildren would go into the tundra in the early autumn, before the snow arrived, to gather cranberries, salmonberries, and blueberries. Since nothing in the tundra grows more than 6 inches off the ground, one sweep of the berry comb could bring in a dozen berries.

Jensen also admires Eskimo ivory artwork, and displays almost 500 objects made from walrus tusks, including knives and forks as well as sculptures of Arctic wildlife. Other museum exhibits he's proud of include stuffed caribou, wolves, elk, a musk ox, and a 1,500-pound polar bear donated by a dentist who used to work

Dr. Paul Jensen and his favorite stuffed musk ox.
Note how both are smiling.

in Kotzebue, Alaska. The dentist now practices in Salem and donated the bear because it scared his patients.

Jensen plans to retire in about five years and then, perhaps, go back up and visit his friends among the Eskimos. Try to visit the Jensen Arctic museum while he's still here, since no museum volunteer can top Jensen's firsthand knowledge of what it was like to live in the sod house that sits in the museum, or to ride in the 27-foot walrus-skin boat.

Paul Jensen Arctic Museum, Western Oregon State College • 590 W Church Street, Monmouth, Oregon 97361 • (503) 838-8468
Admission: Free. **Hours:** Tues–Sat 10am–4pm. **To get there:** Monmouth is west of Salem on 99W. Take Maine or Jackson street west to Stadium Drive. Turn right and continue to Church Street.

High-Tech Housecleaning

NEWBERG
The Gabe Self-Cleaning House

I n the mid-1960s inventor Frances Gabe decided that there were better things to do with her time than clean house—so she started working on a house that would clean itself. Word got out, and Gabe claims that "women from all over the world called, crying and sobbing. Sometimes their husbands would have to hold the phone for them, because they were so gosh-darn pleased that I had finally saved them from housework, they hated it so much." Gabe's self-cleaning house concept hasn't exactly swept the nation, but over the past 30 years she has continued to work on perfecting her designs. Along the way, she's invented dozens of items, including a patented type of upholstery, a self-cleaning organic toilet, self-dusting book jackets, a combination washing machine and cupboard that eliminates the need to have space for both, and a "clothes freshener" intended to bypass the washing machine. But the key to Gabe's self-cleaning house is an item that looks like a fire sprinkler, installed in the ceiling of each room in her house. "Just turn it on and whoosh, the whole room is clean." The "sprinkler" is designed to dispense a cleaning solution over a room that looks pretty much like any room—except that each wooden piece of furniture has eight coats of boat varnish on it, and each room slopes—not noticeably—toward drains in the corners.

Want to see this remarkable house, which Gabe says she built herself for about $18,000 using mostly scavenged and recycled materials? You can; just call and ask for a tour. Gabe will show you both scale models of her inventions and the house itself.

The Gabe Self-Cleaning House • PO Box 901, Newberg, Oregon 97132 • (503) 538-4946
Admission: $5 for adults, no children under 10. **Hours:** By appointment only. **To get there:** Call for directions.

Early Hooverville

Hoover-Minthorn House

While in Newberg, check out another remarkable house—the Hoover-Minthorn House, boyhood home of President Herbert Hoover. Dr. Henry Minthorn was the uncle and, later, the foster father of Hoover. The death of Minthorn's young son prompted him to invite the orphaned, 10-year-old Herbert to come west from Iowa. "Bertie" Hoover lived with his uncle's family in Newberg from 1884 to 1889, and their large house—the oldest still standing in Newberg—has been restored to its condition at that time. Wallpaper patterns are exact replicas, and the original furniture adorns Hoover's bedroom.

The Hoover-Minthorn House • 115 S River Street, Newberg, Oregon 97132 • (503) 538-6629
Admission: $1.50, discounts for children and senior citizens. **Hours:** Mar–Nov: Wed–Sun 1pm–4pm; Dec–Feb: Sat–Sun 1pm–4pm. **To get there:** Newberg is reached from Portland via 99W. Take the left-turn lane to S River Street; the museum is on the corner of 2nd and River streets, adjacent to Hoover Park.

Ride 'em, Cowgirl!

PENDLETON
Pendleton Round-Up
Hall of Fame

Nothing can compete with a rodeo for offering weekend cowpokes an enjoyable and condensed taste of classic Western culture. An afternoon in the grandstands watching steers get roped, bulls get ridden, and cowboys get bucked is a thrilling reminder of an era that is fading all too quickly, as ranches are turned into condominium villages and riders get their roping experience at universities instead of out on the range.

As traditional rodeos go, the Pendleton Round-Up is one of the best. The second-oldest rodeo in the country, it's steeped in history, community traditions, and lore. Begun in 1910 as a local Fourth of July event to offset summertime boredom, the Round-Up now draws more than 50,000 visitors a year to this town of 10,000 ranchers, farmers, and businesspeople. To honor the cowboys, cowgirls, Native American tribes, and townspeople who have helped keep the Pendleton Round-Up a going concern since the beginning, there is the Pendleton Round-Up Hall of Fame, a one-room museum tucked under the arena grandstand, right next to the rollicking bar called the Let 'er Buck Room.

Inside the museum, almost every inch of wall, floor, and support-post space is covered with Round-Up memorabilia

Officials banned women from competing in the Pendleton Round-Up in 1929 after cowgirl Bonnie McCarroll was killed in a fall. (Bonnie survived this tumble.)

dating back to the first Round-Up: angora riding chaps, bull whips, silver-encrusted prize saddles and belt buckles, and pictures of every single rodeo queen and her court since 1910. Right here in the middle of the room is a stuffed horse! This isn't any old horse—it's Warpaint, the famous bucking bronco. Warpaint strikes a classic pose: his teeth are bared and his back legs kick up in the air. To see the kind of damage a horse like this could do, take a close look at the hundreds of photos on the wall titled "Rodeo Wrecks," early snapshots of arena accidents that even today can make you wince and start limping.

The cowboys memorialized here include local ranchers as well as the better-known stars of the rodeo circuit who performed regularly at the Round-Up, including Monty Montana, a trick rider whose skills took him to Hollywood and whose sparkling red show outfit is on display. The Hall of Fame also pays tribute to the small group of cowgirls who rode in the early days at Pendleton, even though in 1929 Round-Up officials banned women from competing in the rodeo's major events after one unlucky cowgirl, Bonnie McCarroll, was killed in a fall from a bucking horse. Women still aren't part of the major events here.

Like the rodeo, the Round-Up Hall of Fame is run by a committee of local volunteers. Many of the museum staffers are old-timers who grew up never missing a Round-Up, so don't be shy about asking them to share their rodeo stories.

Pendleton Round-Up Hall of Fame • 1205 SW Court Avenue, PO Box 609, Pendleton, Oregon 97801 • (503) 276-2553 or (800) 824-1603 (in Oregon); (800) 524-2984 (outside Oregon)
Admission: Free. Hours: Mid-June–mid-Sept: every day, 1pm–4pm. Longer hours during Round-Up Days; other times by appointment. To get there: The rodeo grounds are the biggest thing in town. The Hall of Fame is under the arena grandstand.

Woolly Bully

Umatilla County Historical Society Museum

The Umatilla County Historical Society Museum is located in what was once Pendleton's railway depot. The collection includes items commemorating the Oregon Trail; beadwork and other artifacts from the Cayuse, Umatilla, Walla Walla, and Nez Perce Indians; a working railroad telegraph system; and a display honoring the area's sheep industry and the Pendleton Woolen Mills.

Umatilla County Historical Society Museum • 108 SW Frazer Avenue, PO Box 253, Pendleton, Oregon 97801 • (503) 276-0012
Admission: By donation. **Hours:** Tues–Sat 10am–4pm. **To get there:** From I-84, take exit 210. Drive north towards city center. Turn left on Isaac Avenue and right onto Main Street; the museum is in the old railroad depot across the tracks.

Madison Avenue's Greatest Hits

The American Advertising Museum

Want to know where the phrases "They laughed when I sat down at the piano" or "The skin you love to touch" come from? Need to do research on, say, an early newspaper like *The Pennsylvania Gazette* of the early 1700s? Curious about the beginnings of radio advertising? Dying to see some really, really cool old neon signs? Then the American Advertising Museum is for you. This museum, the first of its kind, opened in 1986. It's housed in a brick building in Portland's Old Town (the former site of Erickson's Café and Concert Hall, which reputedly had the longest bar in the world)—a long way, in short, from Madison Avenue. It illuminates the world of advertising, promotion, and public relations—a world that is often maligned but is also responsible for some of the most memorable items in American pop culture and commerce.

Creating the museum, which is sponsored by the Portland Advertising Federation, has not been an easy job. Advertising is a notoriously fickle industry, and many of its most famous, interesting, or important artifacts have long since been thrown out as useless trash. Collecting what remains is a hit-or-miss proposition; the museum staff is constantly on the prowl for new acquisitions. Still, these holdings are impressive. Among the permanent features in the 6,000-square-foot space: an example of early-American print advertising, circa 1683; vintage outdoor advertising; continuously playing radio commercials (including the first, from 1922); celebrity ads featuring endorsements from the likes of Jack Benny, Ed Wynn, Stan Freberg, Arthur Godfrey, and Bing Crosby; and examples of commercial work from such famous artists as Norman Rockwell, N. C. Wyeth, and Maxfield Parrish.

For anyone who grew up with TV, the museum's collection

of vintage television ads makes for wonderful reminiscing. One of the most requested favorites is the famous ad in which, according to legend, actress Betty Furness pretended she couldn't open a refrigerator door. (In fact, it wasn't Furness who performed—she was sick the day the commercial was shot, and another actress, June Graham, filled in.)

In addition to its permanent holdings, the museum mounts a variety of temporary and traveling exhibits. Typical titles for these shows: "As Good as You Remember: The Original Art from Cream of Wheat Advertising"; "Ethnic Images in Advertising"; and "Claymation: From Mind to Motion" (which highlights working models and other artifacts from the fertile brain of Oscar-winning Portland filmmaker Will Vinton, creator of the popular dancing California Raisins). A large reference library stocked with books, magazines, and audiovisual materials is open to the public.

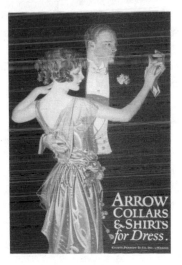

The American Advertising Museum • 9 NW 2nd Avenue, Portland, Oregon 97209 • (503) AAM-0000
Admission: $3. **Hours:** Wed–Fri 11am–5pm, Sat–Sun 12pm–5pm. **To get there**: From I-5 south, follow the signs to City Center and take exit 1A. On Front Avenue, go through three stoplights and make your next right onto 2nd. Go ½ mile, cross

Burnside Street; the museum is on the left in a three-story brick building. From I-5 north, take exit 300B (City Center/Oregon City), stay in the farthest right lane possible, and get off at Morrison Street. At the foot of the exit, go right at the stoplight onto 2nd; go six blocks and cross Burnside; the museum is on the left in a three-story brick building between Burnside and Couch.

Git Along, Little Dogie

PORTLAND
Cowboys Then and Now Museum

Located in the offices of the Oregon Beef Industry Council, this bright, tightly packed museum promises—and delivers—a colorful, historically accurate ride through the evolution of the American cowboy—and, of course, the cattle industry as well. Although the first display features a chart titled "Hamburger History," identifying where various cuts of meat come from, your attention will be quickly drawn to the well-researched story of those rough-and-tumble cowboys of yesteryear.

Museum "host" Alan Winson clearly loves researching cowboy history, and he shares his findings both in conversation with visitors and as he follows the timeline that runs the length of the museum. The timeline traces the cattle industry all the way back to Christopher Columbus, who unloaded the New World's first herd of cattle in Haiti on January 2, 1494. The real roots of the Western cowboy, according to the exhibit, date to the early 1500s, when Spanish ranchers in northern Mexico began branding their cattle and using skilled horsemen to look after their herds. The need for the workers, who eventually became known as cowboys, blossomed throughout America by the mid-1800s, as ranchers began to move large herds of cattle to markets in Kansas, New Mexico, Colorado, and Wyoming.

All those cowboys moving their huge herds of cattle had to stop and eat somewhere, so it's appropriate that one of the museum's major displays is built around a chuckwagon, the vehicle that served as a portable kitchen for cowboys out on the range. The chuckwagon here is 100 years old and comes from a ranch in eastern Oregon. A pair of mannequins dressed in authentic Western wear are part of this vignette. Be sure to be formally introduced to "Zack," the cowboy standing just behind the chuckwagon. He's a rootin', tootin' holographic fella who comes alive to tell you his life story.

Farther along the trail you'll find the cowboy's cryptic alphabet, used to design the brand each ranch used to identify its cattle. The museum displays seven of the oldest branding-iron designs used on Oregon ranches. Also on hand are samples of early barbed wire, a post–Civil War innovation that provided ranchers with a cheap way of keeping livestock from straying too far.

Barbed wire eliminated much of the work previously done by cowboys, but their story doesn't end there. The museum timeline goes on to explore America's continuing fascination with old-time cowboys—in fiction, art, poetry, and, of course, at the movies. Visitors can test their knowledge of "Box Office Buckaroos" at a push-button, light-up display, and one exhibit features Barbara Stanwyck's script from the 1954 film *The Cattle Queen of Montana* (which co-starred that ole cowpoke Ronald Reagan). Other hands-on exhibits include a Western saddle that kids of all ages can climb into, a fully stocked tack room with cowbells to ring, Stetson hats to try on, and plush angora riding chaps to run your hands over. Also on hand are souvenirs from the Pendleton Round-Up, a well-stocked library focusing on Western history and art, and—since the museum is, after all, sponsored by the beef industry—a large cookbook section.

Cowboys Then and Now Museum • 729 NE Oregon Street, Portland, Oregon 97232 • (503) 731-3333
Admission: Free. **Hours:** Wed–Fri 11am–5pm, Sat–Sun 12pm–5pm. **To get there:** The museum is three blocks east of the Oregon Convention Center and two blocks west of Lloyd Center. From the Convention Center on Holladay Street, go to 8th Avenue and turn right. Continue two blocks to NE Oregon Street.

Unbreakable Banks

PORTLAND
Kidd's Toy Museum

Frank Kidd grew up helping in his family's car parts business. He became interested in toy cars only after he'd already put together a collection of full-size antique autos. According to Frank's wife, Joyce, one day about 25 years ago Frank bought some tiny toy cars at an antique-car swap meet; after that, there was no turning back. Today Frank Kidd has a toy collection that any child—and most adults—will envy.

Kidd's collection of almost 8,000 toys features passenger cars, delivery trucks, fire trucks, several hundred motorcycles, and dolls dressed in gas-station uniforms. His toy fascination has also expanded to include trains, planes, toy ray guns and cap guns, railroad memorabilia, and other assorted items. But what Kidd values most is a roomful of mechanical cast-iron banks. His favorite is a bank in the shape of a girl who skips rope when a penny is deposited, but he also has Santas, babies in eggs, clowns sitting on globes, frogs, dogs, and even a big black, red, and yellow Ferris wheel bank. The use of cast iron for toys began in the 1870s, and Kidd considers early mechanical banks to be the best examples of the use of cast iron by American toy manufacturers.

Kidd used to keep his collection in his house, but it grew so large that he began storing it on spare shelves at his auto parts store. Now the walls in the busy front sales area are filled with toys, and so are two first-floor offices. He's even had a storage room remodeled to showcase the cast-iron banks. Until Kidd declared the entire collection a museum, only truck drivers, salespeople, and do-it-yourselfers seeking out car parts stumbled upon it. Charmed, these people would often come back on Saturdays with their family and friends. Now the Kidds hand out bright-yellow brochures and book tours for senior citizens' groups. You can see most of the collection any time the store is open, but the cast-iron banks are up a flight of stairs and shown by appointment only, or if one of the Kidds happens to be around.

If you want to see more, go across the street to a store called Kar Parts at 1327 SE Grand. The Kidds own this store, too, because in the past their suppliers wouldn't let them sell wholesale and retail from the same site. Although those rules have relaxed, the Kidds still keep the two buildings. Half of the second store is filled with displays of tin toys, a giant wooden bellows, license plates, guns, animal skins and mounted animal heads, more toy cars (of course), and a glass case of Second World War armaments. The other half is a retail car parts business.

Kidd's Toy Museum • 1300 SE Grand Avenue, PO Box 14828, Portland, Oregon 97214 • (503) 233-7807

Admission: Free. **Hours:** Mon–Fri 8am–5:30pm, Sat 8am–1pm; other times by appointment. **To get there:** From downtown Portland, cross the Willamette River via the Hawthorne Bridge to Grand Avenue. The museum is located inside Parts Distribution, which is on your right, but since Grand Avenue is one-way in the other direction, you'll need to go up Hawthorne Boulevard a few blocks and swing around to get on Grand Avenue in the right direction.

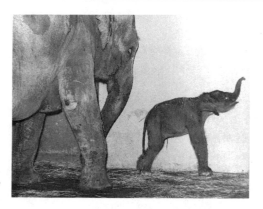

Portland's best-loved pachyderm, Packy, with his mother in 1962.

Packy's Legacy

PORTLAND
The Lilah Callen Holden Elephant Museum, Metro Washington Park Zoo

Elephants have held an important and often revered role in African, Asian, and early European cultures for thousands of years. They've been pressed into service as work animals, as surefooted transportation, and as performers in circuses as early as 3500 B.C. They have also been hunted, almost to extinction, for their ivory tusks.

The first elephant to arrive in America came in April 1796 by boat from Calcutta, and was first placed on exhibit opposite the Governor's Mansion in New York City. After that, it was walked to Philadelphia and Washington, D.C., then back to Boston in time for Christmas, where friendly Bostonians prepared for it an enormous plum pudding (which made the animal sick). In 1812 the elephant was sold to a circus.

Today, elephants don't do much publicity hiking, so most Americans see them only at the circus or a zoo. One particularly good place to observe them is Portland's Washington Park Zoo, which boasts the largest breeding herd of Asian elephants outside their native habitat as well as what may be the only elephant museum in the country.

Most visitors never even notice the museum, perhaps because it's tucked away in a back corner of the zoo; the stucco, gold-domed building is often mistaken for a storage shed. Those who manage to tear themselves away from the live elephants next door will find such artifacts as a giant red elephant tricycle and a large "howdah," or elephant saddle. There are also various examples of art with a pachyderm theme, including three Salvador Dali prints, a painting by Henry Moore titled *Elephant Skull - Plate I*, and African elephant masks made from beads, cloth, and wood. While many items show the role of elephants in art, mythology, and religious ceremonies, several cases demonstrate their role as hunted animals. One is filled with objects made from ivory, and Educational Services manager David Mask hopes to bring from storage hundreds of other ivory objects that have been donated over the years to the museum. Stuffing a case with decorative ivory items with no practical value will, he hopes, alert visitors to the plight of the world's dwindling elephant population.

On a more positive note, Mask says that visitors always spend time at the case filled with Packy paraphernalia. The much-loved Packy was born at Washington Park Zoo in April 1962, and—as the first elephant to be born in the Americas in almost 50 years—became a real celebrity. He was featured in *Life* magazine and in enough newspaper articles to fill a big blue scrapbook.

Mask says that it is no longer unusual for zoos to mix smaller museum-style displays with the live animals. "Zoos need to show the connection between animals, humans, and the planet," he contends. "Otherwise, people won't understand how important it is to protect the place the animals come from."

The Lilah Callen Holden Elephant Museum, Metro Washington Park Zoo • 4001 SW Canyon Road, Portland, Oregon 97221 • (503) 226-1561

Admission: $5 for adults, discounts for children. **Hours:** Every day, 9:30am–closing (varies by season). **To get there:** The zoo is on Highway 26 West, in Washington Park, southwest of downtown Portland.

And Pokey, Too

PORTLAND
Name That Toon and Gumby Museum

N ame That Toon is actually an animation art gallery, but many of the items are not for sale; they're part of what the gallery owners call "the first three-dimensional animation museum ever." The gallery acts as the exclusive dealer for Art Clokey, the creator of the classic 1950s TV character Gumby, and has established itself as the first and only official Gumby Museum. They claim to own all extant materials from the Gumby television show and movie, including sets, props, and clay models of Gumby and his family—and, of course, Gumby's pony pal, Pokey. True Gumby fans will be delighted to see the original saloon set, the house next door to Gumby's parents' house, and a re-creation of Gumby's magical metamorphosis from a mere round lump of clay into the bendy green guy we all know and love.

Also on display are original sets and clay sculptures used to make the world-famous Viewmaster stereo reels, other animation-related treats such as the Poppin' Fresh Doughboy, and a large number of clay figures from the Portland-based studios of Will Vinton, the Academy Award–winning artist behind Claymation and the creator of such characters as the California Raisins. Exhibits change periodically, but Gumby and the Raisins are always there.

Name That Toon and Gumby Museum • 1039 NW Glisan Street, Portland, Oregon 97209 • (503) 222-1219
Admission: Free. Hours: Mon–Sat 10am–5pm Sun 12pm 5pm. To get there. Name That Toon is a few blocks north of Union Station.

Science Is Fun

Oregon Museum of Science and Industry

The Oregon Museum of Science and Industry recently moved from its cramped facilities next door to Portland's Washington Park Zoo to a $40 million complex three times larger across the river and under the Marquam Bridge. Gone are some of our favorites: the walk-through human heart, the Humpty Dumpty chick hatchery, and the pair of human lungs attached to a respirator that revealed what smoking can do to your

insides. Back by popular demand, as part of expanded exhibits on "Designer Genes" and the "Whole Body," are the two-headed, two-tailed lamb and the popular Transparent Woman.

It will take several visits to see the six new exhibit halls, the participatory labs and activity centers, the OMNIMAX theater with its 10,000-square-foot screen, the planetarium, the submarine, and the many touring exhibits planned for the new OMSI.

Visit the Earth Science Hall to find out how geology, weather, biology, and other earthly elements work together as a single system. Then move on to the wild Rube Goldberg–style Recyclotron, a contraption of chutes, pathways, and mechanical connections designed to demonstrate the global impact of your everyday decisions about garbage.

Move from garbage to genes in the "Designer Genes" exhibit in the Life Science Hall, where you can practice making the ethical decisions made possible by today's—and tomorrow's—modern technology. The exhibit poses questions on biomedical and ethical issues such as euthanasia and transplants, then asks you to vote on what you would do in given situations.

A potentially controversial exhibit in the Life Sciences Hall, and perhaps not appropriate for very young children, is the display featuring 42 human embryos in different stages of development. Although it's modeled after an exhibit that's been popular at Chicago's Museum of Science and Industry since 1939, museum officials emphasize that the development of each fetus here was stopped by "natural causes," not abortion, and that the specimens all came from university collections.

Everywhere you turn there's something to do or try, and it all helps to demystify complex scientific concepts. Many exhibits are truly interactive, encouraging visitors to test model cars in a wind tunnel, see how a building they design will stand up to an earthquake, feel what it's like to ride a sailboard, or practice efficient loading of a transport ship. Attached to each hall (Earth Science, Life Science, Information Science, Physical Science, and Space) are staffed laboratories, so if you want to learn more than an exhibit has to offer, you can go into the lab and get a test that gives you a problem to solve.

Oregon Museum of Science and Industry • 1945 SE Water Avenue, Portland, Oregon 97214 • (503) 797-4000
Admission: $6.50 for adults, discounts for children. Hours: Winter: Sat–Wed 9:30am–5:30pm, Thur Fri 9:30am–9pm; summer: Sat–Wed 9:30am–7pm, Thurs–Fri 9:30am–9pm; closed Christmas. To get there: Take I-5 to Water Avenue (exit 300 B). Go south on Water Avenue and follow signs to OMSI parking.

The Country's First Policewoman

PORTLAND
Portland Police Museum

The staffs at urban police stations don't have much time these days to show groups of schoolchildren around, and jail cells are too full to assume there will be an empty one that visitors can get their pictures taken in. To help fill the gap, and to present the history and heritage of the Portland Police Department, the Portland Police Historical Society sponsors a museum on an upper floor of the city's Justice Center, which also houses several floors of jail space. You'll know you're in the right place when you spot the 5½-foot tall neon police badge at the front door.

Museum director Rob Aichele is a retired police officer whose father was a police officer and whose son is also a police officer. So, in a way, Aichele himself is part of police history. He says that many items here were donated in 1976, when the department put out a call for memorabilia it could "take custody of." They were given enough material to fill the museum.

Lola G. Baldwin, the country's first policewoman, was hired in Portland in 1905.

Besides documenting local police history, the museum shows the side of police activity that citizens normally never get to see. One popular showcase contains safecracking items used in actual burglaries and left at the scene of the crime—drills, crowbars of all sizes, gloves, fuses, blasting caps, and even a tiny, cushioned bottle of nitroglycerine. One small room is filled with confiscated weapons, including all varieties of pistols and shotguns, meat hooks, and large, sharp scissors.

The Portland police claim some firsts. The first police radio system in the United States was installed in Portland in 1932. In 1905 Portland hired the first policewoman. Her name was Lola G. Baldwin and her career began when Portland hosted the Lewis and Clark Exposition. Word had come West that many young girls had vanished during previous such fairs in the East, so the Portland Police Department hired Baldwin for $75 a month to help "fight the evils of the day." Baldwin was in charge of coordinating an army of volunteers who met all incoming trains and boats and led visitors "in the right direction," trying not to lose too many young women to "procurers and madams of Portland's bawdy houses." By 1908 an entire Women's Protective Division had been established, with Lola Baldwin as superintendent.

Kids love this museum, and several exhibits are designed especially for them. One highlight is the human-size mannequin of "Mr. McGruff," the crime-fighting, trenchcoat-sporting dog. Push a button and he'll sing an antidrug rap song. Kids (or grownups) can step into an old jail cell and get their picture taken. There's also a climbable Harley-Davidson police motorcycle complete with sidecar, flashing lights, and crackling police radio.

Portland Police Museum • Justice Center, 1111 SW 2nd Avenue, Portland, Oregon 97204 • (503) 796-3019
Admission: Free. Hours: Mon–Thurs 10am–3pm. To get there: The Justice Center is on SW 2nd Avenue, at the foot of the Hawthorne Bridge, between SW Main and SW Madison streets. The museum is on the 16th floor in room 1682.

Kitchen Culture

Apron Exhibit,
Powell's City of Books,

Aprons have been with us ever since Adam and Eve decided to cover themselves with fig leaves. They have since evolved from protecting our modesty to protecting our clothes, and sometimes take on rich symbolic meaning: Egyptian pharaohs wore them as signs of royal power, and sculpted figures of the ancient Minoan fertility goddess depict her sporting a sacred apron. In the Middle Ages women began draping aprons across their laps at mealtime and then began to wear them all day (the word "apron" derives from the old French *napperon,* or napkin). Aprons were eventually adopted by men as well, and in time came to represent particular classes and trades; working women in the 1500s wore heavy white aprons, English barbers wore checkered ones, and butchers had blue-and-white stripes.

More than ten years ago Anne Hughes began buying aprons at yard sales for a dime or a quarter apiece. Many of them were homemade and, to Hughes, embodied messages about kitchen, family, and food. Friends started bringing her aprons as gifts, and now she figures she has about 600. Some of the aprons in her collection are too delicate ever to have been useful in the kitchen, and others were clearly never worn.

Hughes keeps most of her aprons stacked in boxes at home, but she has numerous examples of rescued kitchen culture decorating the upper walls of her coffeeshop inside the voluminous

Powell's bookstore. Hughes says the bookstore is an unusual but perfect place for an apron display, because "the books are so rectangular and the aprons are wild and colorful and give you some relief." Indeed, with 57 pairs of apron ties stretched out like beckoning arms, the aprons seem to be dancing above the serious, hushed browsers.

Hughes changes the display "whenever [the aprons] get too dirty." Among the current crop of vintage 1950s aprons, we saw a set of matching mother-daughter aprons, a definite home-economics class project (with "The Beatles" cross-stitched on one pocket), and one of Hughes's favorites—a chiffon, see-through, red "cocktail" apron.

Powell's Books • 1005 W Burnside, Portland, Oregon 97209 • (503) 228-4651 or (800) 878-READ
Admission: Free. Hours: Mon–Sat 9am–11pm, Sun 9am–9pm. To get there: Powell's fills an entire block. The main entrance is at the corner of 10th and W Burnside, where you can pick up a map of the store. The aprons are in the Anne Hughes Coffee Room, to the left of the entrance.

Sanitizing by Suction

PORTLAND
The Vacuum Cleaner Museum

In a back room of Stark's Vacuum Cleaner Sales and Service, visitors can find the West Coast's only vacuum cleaner museum. Although Stark's is one of the largest stores in the country devoted exclusively to vacuum cleaners, the entrance to its singular collection of vintage machines is far from flashy. "There isn't a sign," warns company president John Stark. "When you see the real old funny-looking vacuum cleaners, you're here."

Along the walls of the long, narrow room are 86 devices that "sanitize by suction," neatly arranged and each bearing a typewritten manila tag detailing the model name, year of production, special features, and degree of cleaning ability. The Regina Model 59, for instance, which came complete with its own muffler, is labeled: "Best upright straight suction vacuum ever built."

Harold Gray, who was once the company's board chairman, collected the vacuum cleaners; some of them were donated outright, but many arrived at Stark's by way of customers who brought in ancient machines, hoping to trade them in or have them repaired.

The earliest models are pre-electric, mechanically operated affairs that look a little like clam guns or car mufflers. They worked, after a fashion, when the user manually pushed and pulled a piston rod and bellows; mostly, they succeeded in stirring the dust around. "I don't think they picked up hardly any dirt," Stark admits, "it was a status symbol." But with the era of electricity (the first successful electric cleaner was introduced by Beach in 1908), the vacuum cleaner came into its own. Stark's museum traces the evolution of each successive refinement: dual rear wheels, carpet-depth adjusters, rubber-tooth rug agitators, easy-access fan chambers, tilt-latch handle locks, cloth bags, quick-release dirt trays, revolving brushes, clutches, double clutches, headlights, and knuckle-knobbed handle forks.

The names of the machines are poetry in themselves, evoking a bygone era of consumer advertising: Electro-Sweep, Silent-aire, Royal, Cinderella, Airway, and Cadillac. The Haley's Comet, which dates from the 1960s, has a little jingle inside its lid: "The Age of Space, the Rocket Race, push-button leisure day. Be the first to clean your jet-set home the Haley's Comet way." Others have somewhat more prosaic names—the Dirtmaster, for example. This ill-starred model was manufactured for only two years, 1937 and 1938, and its tag notes that it was "heavy, hard to use. Very few were sold." Maybe it just suffered from a poor choice of name.

Stark's Vacuum Cleaner Sales and Service • 107 NE Grand Avenue, Portland, Oregon 97232 • (503) 232-4101
Admission: Free. Hours: Mon, Fri 8am–8pm, Tues–Thurs 8am–6pm, Sat 9am–6pm. To get there: From downtown Portland cross the Burnside Bridge. Grand Avenue is over the bridge, and Stark's is on your left.

Almost Human

PORTLAND
Van Calvin's Manikin Restoration

Some of the naked plaster bodies posing in the windows at Van Calvin's mannequin shop appear so lifelike that passersby come back two or three times to look again. One man was so shocked by what he thought he saw there that he threatened to throw a bomb in the window.

Although this is not officially a museum, the storage rooms at Van Calvin's hold literally all the pieces that compose mannequin history: fingers, heads, hands, arms, and torsos, and almost 1,000 fully formed plaster, *papier mâché*, and fiberglass bodies. Even with one of the staff as your tour guide, walking through the silent crowds of naked fiberglass men, women, and children, all of whom appear to have been frozen in midstride while staring straight at you or off into space, can be a little eerie.

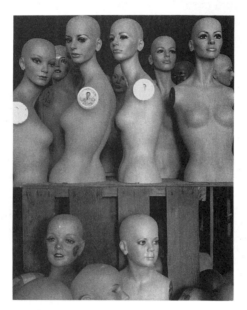

The models from different eras show how, over time, faces and body styles have changed. Whereas early mannequins were plump, rigid figures with elongated necks, plain expressions, and hands held straight to their sides, today's "silent salesgirls," as Van Calvin calls them, are much more lifelike. These days the female mannequins have bumps in all the right places, tiny waists, and lots of makeup. Their poses are more contemporary, too. These modern-day mannequins might be running, swimming, riding a bicycle, eating, or even taking a bath.

Calvin ("Van" is her first name) says that many of the models have their own personalities. Giuseppe, who is often rented for grocery-store displays, is one of her favorites because he's a nice, good-looking guy and a good worker. But she says some mannequins seem to have nasty dispositions, and one department-store display worker insisted on trading in one model because it reminded him of his ex-wife.

Calvin tells some great stories from her 30-plus years of re-painting and restoring dummies. She's re-created bullet-ridden heads for the district attorney's office and turned standard models from her storeroom into movie-star lookalikes. She even knows of a minister who performed a wedding ceremony for one of her customers and a special-order mannequin bride.

Due to failing health, Calvin recently turned the business over to Russ Varner, who promises to continue the sometimes-shocking window-display tradition, to learn the best of Van Calvin's stories, and to share some of his own.

Van Calvin's Manikin Restoration • 16950 NW Saint Helens Road, Portland, Oregon 97231 • (503) 621-3007

Admission: Free. **Hours:** By appointment only. **To get there:** The shop is 2 miles past the Sauvie Island Bridge on US 30 West.

The Church of Elvis

PORTLAND
Where's The Art!! A Gallery of Art for the Smart

I n need of a little spiritual guidance? Why not employ the services of Dr. Justin D. Nick-of-Time, the World's Cheapest Psychic? Better yet, why not pray before the Holy Computer

Monitor of the Church of Elvis? It only costs a quarter, you receive a free prize, and you'll feel ever so much better. Best of all, you can worship the King 24 hours a day here.

The good doctor and the Church of Elvis are found in the windows of Where's The Art!!, a tiny, cluttered artist's storefront in Portland's Old Town. Owner Stephanie G. Pierce (an ex-lawyer) describes herself as "artist to the stars, confirmed semifinalist, celebrity spokesmodel, minister, and hostette." She claims, no doubt correctly, that hers is the world's first 24-hour coin-operated art gallery.

Imagine a 3-D Lynda Barry cartoon and you'll get an idea of the storefront displays at Where's The Art!! The Church of Elvis window features—what else?—a host of Elvis memorabilia surrounding a computer screen, with messages in Pierce's inimitable scrawl adorning every available surface. Drop a quarter in the slot by the door and the computer screen lights up. Press a button and all hell breaks loose: weird primeval noises, strange images, jumbles of words and phrases. None of it makes an awful lot of sense, but there you go. Just watch the colored lights, read the text, and listen. Then wait for your FREE PRIZE to pop out at the end—perhaps a tiny, stapled-together pamphlet called *The Book of Elvis*, or your own psychic roadmap. It really is a church, too; for a nominal fee, Pierce (a legally ordained mail-order minister) will perform weddings, complete with an ultra-tacky procession up and down the block (you can also get a "non-binding" wedding via the computer).

Asked to sum up the aesthetic philosophy behind her art, Pierce says, "If it's not tragic and spectacular at the same time, we don't want to do it."

Where's The Art!! A Gallery of Art for the Smart • 219 SW Ankeny Street, Portland, Oregon 97204 • (503) 226-3671

Admission: 25 cents. **Hours:** Storefront coin-op machines operate 24 hours a day.

To get there: Ankeny is a narrow street in Portland's Old Town District; Where's The Art!! is across from the Oyster Bar on SW Ankeny, between 2nd and 3rd avenues.

The Talking Tree

World Forestry Center

Trees are one of the Northwest's most valued natural resources. Don't just take our word for it—at the World
Forestry Center you can hear it straight from the horse's
mouth, or, to be more correct, direct from the tree's limbs. In the
center of the main exhibit hall a talking tree acts as "host," giving
visitors a quick introduction to the topic of trees and the forest environment. It's really an audiotape you trigger by pressing a button, but if you're not too self-conscious to be seen listening to a
tree talk, you'll get a review of tree parts, from hardwood to bark,
and learn that it would take 200 gallons of water for this tree to
survive in the forest.

Exhibits include hands-on and push-button displays detailing
logging practices and logging equipment, and information on efforts
to keep forests healthy. On the second floor are vertical showcases filled with wooden plates. When Jim Langdon retired from

the U.S. Forest Service he decided to make plates out of as many different woods as he could get his hands on. He did a very complete job, and nearly 400 of the 600 plates he made are here.

Another far-ranging wood exhibit is the Jesup Collection of Wood, assembled in the late 1800s by Morris Jesup, a wealthy banker who was once president of the American Museum of Natural History. Jesup hired a dendrologist, or tree specialist, to gather more than 500 tree samples, representing all the significant species of North American trees. The 100-ton collection took 12 years to complete and was originally shown at the American Museum.

The Forestry Center received the collection in 1964, the same year the old Forestry Building (built in 1905) was destroyed by fire. This giant log cabin, built of old-growth Douglas fir, each log 5 feet in diameter, had been the intended home for the Jesup Collection. Luckily, the two boxcars full of the tree samples hadn't arrived in Portland when the fire broke out. When the new Forestry Center was built in 1971, it became home to the entire 505-piece collection.

There's one more "wooden wonder" you don't want to miss. On the second floor, look for what the Forestry Center calls its "Armed Willow." This willow tree grew around a .22-caliber rifle left in a bend of the tree, leaving only a small portion of the rifle visible.

NOTE: If fund-raising efforts succeed, the Forestry Center plans to shut down for renovations in January 1994 for up to six months, so call ahead.

World Forestry Center • 4033 SW Canyon Road, Portland, Oregon 97221 • (503) 228-1367
Admission: $3 for adults, discounts for children and senior citizens. **Hours:** Summer: every day 9am–5pm; after Labor Day: every day 10am–5pm; closed Christmas. **To get there:** The Forestry Center is outside downtown Portland on Highway 26 West, near the Metro Washington Park Zoo.

Elizabeth Taylor Changed Costumes Here

World Famous Fantastic Museum

Probably the unlikeliest location for a museum of curiosities is sleepy Redmond, Oregon, where a well-to-do and "semiretired" real-estate man named Jim Schmit has assembled a 17,000-square-foot warehouse of weird and wacky items. The Fantastic Museum is only one of Schmit's attempts to bring some glitz to eastern Oregon; another of his projects is the restoration of a dilapidated resort called Hunter's Hot Springs, where he installed what he believes to be the world's largest collection of outhouses—about 25 of them. Much of the material at the Fantastic Museum was purchased from the Jones Fantastic Museum, which those of us who were at an impressionable age in 1962 will remember fondly from the Seattle World's Fair. But a great deal more has been added by Schmit, who started collecting oddball stuff as a high school student in Puyallup and later as a Lake Tahoe businessman.

Among the wonders at the Fantastic Museum: a full-size mechanical elephant, a stunt car with backseat drive used by Laurel and Hardy, Elizabeth Taylor's dressing-room trailer from the *Cleopatra* set, an 8-½-foot "mummified Viking" named Olaf, an instrument that is alleged to be Elvis's first guitar, and over a million buttons. There's also a collection of late nineteenth- and early twentieth-century mechanical piggybanks, a group of antique animated toys, a 1932 TV set (the Jenkins Commercial Reflecting Televisor) that plays two hours of vintage commercials on tape, and a selection of pipes, golf clubs, and fishing poles that once belonged to Bing Crosby. Schmit displays several funhouses, mirrors, laughing ladies, arcade machines from circuses, and a few of his 50-odd vintage cars (including the Caddy that took Eisenhower to his first inaugural ball). Eclectic and mind-boggling.

World Famous Fantastic Museum • 33905 S Highway 97, Redmond, Oregon 97756 • (503) 923-0000
Admission: $5 for adults, discounts for children. **Hours:** Every day 9am–9pm. **To get there:** The museum is on the east side of US 97 and Airport Way.

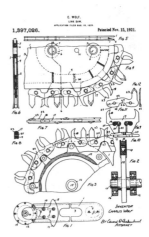

Where Chain Saws Go to Die

ROSEBURG
Hunt's Chain Saw Museum

It's not surprising that there are several chain-saw collections in the forested Northwest. In fact, the first truly practical chain saw was invented in Portland in 1920 by Charlie Wolf of Peninsula Iron Works.

Syl and Gary Hunt repair and sell chain saws at their shop in Roseburg, Oregon, but over the years they've accumulated almost 60 saws that hang around the store (literally). The Hunts get lots of visitors, although they don't claim to have the oldest, the biggest, or the most powerful saws. They always take time to chat with guests, Gary said, because they like finding out where people are from, and "that way we don't have to read the newspapers."

The World's Largest Hairball

ST. BENEDICT
Abbey Museum, Mount Angel
Abbey and Seminary

There has been a Benedictine presence at Mount Angel since the 1880s, when Father Adelhelm Odermatt, a Swiss theologian, arrived and built a chapel. The present Benedictine abbey has many unusual features, including a library designed by Alvar Aalto and a rare-books collection, visible to the public from behind glass, that includes a fifth-century Bible in Frankish, a medieval German tongue. But what makes the abbey really special to us is its museum.

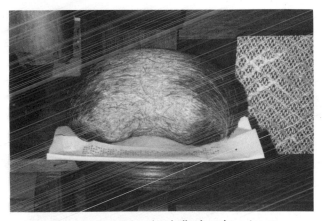

At 2½ pounds, this hog hairball takes the prize at the Mount Angel Abbey.

Father Nathan, who is the unofficial curator of this eclectic museum, is amazed at the bizarre assortment of memorabilia that has ended up here. He is also clearly delighted and "hopefully not too irreverent" when he shows off the rare religious artifacts that share cramped floor, ceiling, and wall space with bizarre twists of nature, stuffed animals, and hand-carved souvenirs from around the world.

Until recently, all the church-related artifacts were displayed unceremoniously cheek-by-jowl with the five bears, the bison, the deer, the raccoon, and the many other stuffed specimens left over from the abbey's natural science classes. Now efforts are under way to divide the one-room museum into two sections, one a bit more solemn than the other. But questions remain: On which side should they place the 11½-inch ear of corn grown on the abbey farm in 1950? Or the bent propeller blade from a fighter plane that crashed on a nearby butte back in 1947? Or the piece of cow spine belonging to the single victim of that crash? These and other treasures were either gathered by the monks themselves or donated by townspeople and friends of the abbey.

Why would people leave such things to a monastery? Perhaps, Father Nathan speculates, because monasteries have been the sites of some of the world's first museums. Also, he believes, "because places like this have staying power." Although the abbey really wants to collect religious objects, it's the "offbeat collectobilia" that keeps pouring in, Father Nathan says. He points to the bottom shelf of a showcase, where two stuffed calves rest peacefully—including one that was born in Tillamook, Oregon, in 1932, with two bodies and one head. Father Nathan says that the calves aren't so unusual; in the past ten years he's turned down at least three two-headed calves and numerous offers of stuffed pet cats. Other donations to the abbey include a cross section of a piece of underwater electric cable and a bullet found two days after Custer's famous last battle.

But the really outstanding part of the Mount Angel Abbey museum is its collection of hairballs. One cardboard box holds five large, brown specimens, each the size of a softball and equally round and smooth, taken from the stomachs of five different cows. Beside the box sits a hairy yam-shaped thing that weighs 2½ pounds. It was found in the stomach of a 300-pound hog at a meatpacking plant. A Portland meat inspector declared it the largest hairball ever found.

Abbey Museum, Mount Angel Abbey and Seminary • St Benedict, Oregon 97373 • (503) 845-3030
Admission: Free. **Hours:** Mon–Sat 9am-12pm and 1pm–5pm, Sun 10am–12pm and 1pm–5pm. **To get there:** Take I-5 to the Silverton exit and go east through Woodburn on Route 214 to Mount Angel. Follow the signs to the abbey. The museum is located in the basement of the Abbey House; ask for the key at the switchboard.

A Tribute to the Erector Set

SALEM
Gilbert House Children's Museum

For nearly 100 years, kids have whiled away long, rainy afternoons building cranes, trucks, and Ferris wheels with the Erector Set—a toy whose fun-with-science attitude was a radical departure from the simpler wooden building blocks and hobbyhorses of previous times. Now you and your young friends can visit a museum dedicated to the man who invented this toy for young engineers.

The childhood of A. C. Gilbert, who was born in Salem in 1884, was marked by a fascination with magic and gadgets. As a student at Yale, he supported himself by performing magic shows and making boxed sets of "ready-made" tricks. In 1911, while riding a train, Gilbert noticed new power lines being built. He later wrote, "I saw steel girder after steel girder being erected [and I thought] how fascinated boys might be in building things out of

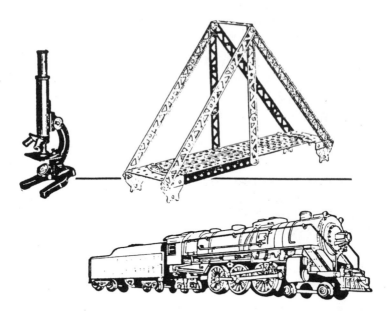

girders." Gilbert introduced the Erector Set to the public in 1913; it was an instant success—30 million sets sold in its first 20 years alone—and Gilbert went on to create dozens of other "toys that teach."

As you can imagine, the emphasis at Gilbert House is on Big Fun Through Science. The museum is housed in two restored Victorian homes (one was Gilbert's uncle's and the other was recently moved adjacent to it). Nominally, it caters to children, from toddlers to teens, but we think just about everyone will find it intriguing. As shop manager Nancy Whiteman says, "Parents get just about as involved as the kids do."

Nearly everything here is hands-on. There's the giant bubble machine (pull a cord and a giant bubble comes up around you), the theater room (a stage and tons of costumes and puppets), and the inventor's workshop (a real working crane! Gears, levers, and pulleys galore!). There's the "Kidspace" room, just for toddlers—if you can pass under the teeny arch, you can play inside. Then there's the Natural History room, which includes a computerized forestry game, a beehive in the wall behind safety glass, and an ant farm. Also a "Chain Reaction" room (drop a ball down a chute or knock over a domino and watch how chain reactions work), a roomful of toys, clothes, and furniture from different cultures (always in flux), and another devoted to musical instruments. Who can resist exhibits with titles like "Good and Gooey" or "Colorful Chemistry"?

The only area where look-but-don't-touch rules apply is the Gilbert Room, upstairs in the original building, where you *are* permitted to play with the Erector Set in the middle of the room, but the rest of Gilbert's legacy is behind glass. Here you'll find examples of many of his 150-odd other inventions as well: American Flyer trains and his popular microscope, weather station, magic trick, and chemistry sets, as well as stuff for grownups, like the "Polar Cub" portable electric fan, the pre-Farrah blow dryer, and the pre-Cuisinart kitchen mixer.

Gilbert House Children's Museum • 116 Marion Street NE, Salem, Oregon 97301 • (503) 371-3631
Admission: $3; children under 10 must be accompanied by an adult. Hours: June 23–Mar 24: Tues–Sat 10am–5pm, Sun 12pm–4pm; Mar 25–June 22: also open first two Mondays of June for school field trips. To get there: The museum is on the downtown Salem Riverfront, between the bridges. From the Front Street bypass, enter the Riverfront via Court Street on the south or Union Street on the north.

Bible Study and Falcon Mummies

SALEM
Prewitt-Allen Museum of Middle Eastern Archaeology, Western Baptist College

The falcon mummies and the falcon casket, dating back to about 3500 B.C., are "not everyone's cup of tea," warns acting curator Richard Muntz. Still, it's the exhibit kids like

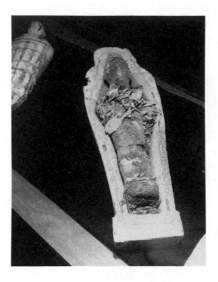

This 5,000-year-old falcon mummy was wrapped in the form of Osiris, in the same way the pharoahs were.

best. Look for it in the Egyptian Room. The mummies are wrapped in the same manner that the late pharaohs were, in the form of Osiris, the god of the dead. The falcon-shaped casket is the symbol of Horus, the god of resurrection. Together with alabaster canopic jars designed to hold and protect a deceased person's lungs, the artifacts show different styles of animal mummification and illustrate the sacred role early Egyptians assigned to many birds and animals.

The museum was originally developed to complement Bible archaeology courses and Middle Eastern study classes at Western Baptist College. However, by building a collection that includes personal and religious items from the cultures and periods described in the Bible, the college has ended up with one of the West Coast's most impressive archaeological museums. You'll find pieces dating back to the Middle Bronze Age and from every archaeological age up to the Byzantine period, including 2,000-year-old olive-oil–burning clay lamps; an eighteenth-century Torah or synagogue scroll; the earliest examples of writing on stone, clay, cloth, and papyrus; and hundreds of other unusual items. Much of the collection was donated by the two men for whom the museum is named: Robert Allen and Frank Prewitt, the museum's late curator.

Prewitt-Allen Museum of Middle Eastern Archaeology, Western
Baptist College • 5000 Deer Park Drive SE, Salem, Oregon 97301 •
(503) 375-7016 or (503) 581-8600 extension 2201
Admission: Free. Hours: School year (late Aug–May): Mon–Fri 7:30am–9pm, Sat
10:30am–4:30pm, Sun 2pm–5pm; summer: Mon-Fri 8am–4pm; call to confirm
hours, as they're often short-staffed in summer. To get there: From I-5 south take
the Highway 22 exit. Turn east on Highway 22, and almost immediately exit to the
right on Lancaster Drive. Travel south on Lancaster past the Marion County Cor-
rectional Facility and turn right on Deer Park Drive. Turn left at the campus's main
entrance. Van Gilder Hall, which houses the museum, is the large building to the
left of the entrance drive.

This six-story shell tower has glass
windows, a hinged door, and little
cows, people, sheep, horses, and
dogs glued to the ledges.

The Seashell Tower

SEASIDE
Seaside Museum and
Historical Society

The Seaside Museum is a healthy reminder that Lewis and
Clark weren't the first to find this choice coastal area. It features a large display of artifacts dating from A.D. 230 found
by the Smithsonian Institution at a dig south of Seaside, along with
paintings, photographs, and artifacts from the local Clatsop Indians.
A small sign notes that in 1805, just before Lewis and Clark's visit,
an estimated 40,000 Clatsops lived in the area, but that just 100
years later, in 1905, the last full-blooded Clatsop in Seaside died.
In 1806 Meriwether Lewis and William Clark broke out of
the woods and gazed upon the Pacific Ocean at the sight of what

became the resort town of Seaside. The view prompted Clark to write in his journal: ". . . beheld the grandest and most pleasing prospect which my eyes ever surveyed, in my frount a boundless Ocean; to the N. and N.E. the coast as far as my sight could be extended, the Seas rageing with emence waves and breaking with great force." The intrepid duo had enjoyed many unbelievable experiences by then, but even these two couldn't have imagined that less than a century later the spot would become a major tourist destination, complete with boardwalk, arcades, and food stands hawking corndogs and saltwater taffy.

Seaside has been a tourist mecca since 1900, and the museum celebrates that fact with pictures of the grand old hotels, a beachside bathhouse, and even the door from the suite in which John F. Kennedy stayed on August 3, 1959, at the Seasider Hotel, shortly before he became president. The museum also displays photographs and descriptions of the "Daddy Train," the nickname given to the Astoria and Columbia River Railway, which completed its route between the Willamette Valley and Seaside in 1898. From 1898 to 1952 this train enabled fathers who worked in Portland to go to Seaside on Friday nights and spend summer weekends with their wives and children who were staying at cottages rented out by the season. Meeting the "Daddy Train" and seeing it off again on Sunday night was a summertime tradition. By 1937 the Sunset Highway between Portland and the coast was completed, and the railroad lost passengers to the automobile. The last train to Seaside ran in 1952.

Small summer homes were everywhere in Seaside, and the museum received one of the turn-of-the-century cottages about ten years ago. The 1893 building was in such bad shape after being moved the few blocks to the museum that the historical society nearly had it demolished, but volunteers came forward to help restore it inside and out, and it now sits sweetly next to the museum with a white picket fence and flowers on the porch.

Seaside Museum and Historical Society • 570 Necanicum Drive, PO Box 1024, Seaside, Oregon 97138 • (503) 738-7065

Found Underground

SWEET HOME
White's Electronic Museum

I n 1950 Kenneth White was using a Geiger counter to search for uranium to sell to the U.S. government for use in atomic bombs and reactors. The machine required the user to wear headphones, so White didn't hear the rattlesnake he was about to step on until it was almost too late. That close call led him to invent and manufacture a Geiger counter, and later a series of metal detectors, that had speakers instead of headphones. White, who recently died, became known as the Henry Ford of the metal detector industry; today his company accounts for a third of the $75 million national metal detector market.

While many of us are familiar with the metal detectors used by amateur and professional treasure-hunters, we were surprised to learn that they're also used in police and FBI investigations, and installed in bakeries and large manufacturing plants to detect nuts and bolts that may fall into food products. One hospital requested a metal-detecting machine to determine if any metal instruments were left inside patients after operations.

Over the years White's manufacturing plant in Sweet Home has accumulated quite a collection of items discovered with metal detectors. White even had an extra room built to hold what is now known as White's Electronic Museum. Here a wide variety of metal detectors are displayed alongside Geiger counters dating back to the 1950s (including the model White was using on the day he encountered the rattlesnake) and artifacts found over the years with the aid of his detectors. Highlights of the collection include old buttons, guns, cash boxes, Civil War medals and other war memorabilia, swords, silverware, coins, gold nuggets, jewelry, and cannons, anchors, and other artifacts from early shipwrecks.

White's Electronic Museum • 1101 Pleasant Valley Road, Sweet Home, Oregon 97386 • (503) 367-2138
Admission: Free. **Hours:** Mon–Fri 8am–4pm. **To get there:** Follow signs from Route 20.

A Resting Place for Blimps

TILLAMOOK
Blimp Hangar Museum

These days we're most familiar with blimps that tow advertising signs overhead or provide bird's-eye camera views during large sporting events. But blimps—lighter-than-air craft—have a long history of military use in both America and Europe. During the Second World War they were an important part of the United States naval fleet. Eight of these giant balloons were stationed at Tillamook in two cavernous hangars. To accommodate varying wind conditions, each hangar was oriented in a different direction. Steel was in high demand elsewhere during the war, so the hangers (1,072 feet long and 170 feet tall) were made of salt-treated, fire-resistant lumber.

The job of the Tillamook blimp fleet was to patrol for enemy submarines from Northern California to the Strait of Juan de Fuca, to escort convoys in Puget Sound, and to trail targets for fighter plane practice. The Navy was conscientious about keeping good relations with the community and, according to museum notes, made quick reparations when "a cow was accidentally sandbagged or a barn cupola damaged by a low-flying blimp." By 1948 the Navy had no more use for the immense hangars smack in the middle of Oregon dairyland, so it leased the "blimp base," as it's known locally, to Tillamook County.

Today the Port of Tillamook Bay owns the base and uses the hangars to display blimps, blimp base memorabilia, and items left over from the now-defunct company that created the ingenious but curious-looking Cyclo-Crane, a hybrid blimp with a motor, four wings, and a tail. The Cyclo-Crane was designed to replace more expensive heavy-lift helicopters in remote logging areas. The company's demise sorely disappointed the U.S. Forest Service, several lumber companies, and even the U.S. Defense Department, which together had invested more than $8 million in the log-lifting blimp experiment.

The blimps on display now include a small test version of the Cyclo-Crane; a commercially operated advertising blimp; a General Electric aerostat blimp once used for radar surveillance along the Mexican border; and a Second World War barrage balloon. The hard-to-spot steel cables hanging off this last blimp were designed to deter enemy aircraft.

The identical blimp hangars at Tillamook are listed in the *Guinness Book of World Records* as the largest free-span wooden structures in the world. Unfortunately they'll have to revise that listing, because in August 1992 a roaring straw-fed arson fire demolished one of them. Although the 7,600 tons of straw being stored in that hangar were insured, the hangar itself was not. Luckily, the other hangar, the one that houses the museum, remains standing.

**Blimp Hangar Museum • 4000 Blimp Boulevard, Tillamook, Oregon
97141 • (503) 842-1130**
Admission: $2. **Hours:** Mid-May–Oct: every day, 10am–6pm; Nov–mid-May:
Sat–Sun and holidays; longer hours are planned, so call ahead. **To get there:** From
Tillamook, take Route 101 South 1½ miles out of town; turn left at the flashing
yellow light and follow the signs to the Blimp Museum. Even if it's raining you should
be able to see a huge, silver building off to your right across the farmland—a building so large that it could only hold, well, a blimp (or two!).

A Two-Headed Dinosaur

TILLAMOOK
Tillamook County Pioneer
Museum

One tiny brown leather memo book, with pages that hold no
more than a few words each, can tell a visitor more about
the spirit and determination of the pioneers who came to
the Tillamook County area than many of the other 35,000 artifacts in this museum. The fragile, worn booklet belonged to Sara

Perkins, an Oregon pioneer who left Illinois with her family in 1853 to head for the Pacific Northwest. She survived the treacherous trip, but some in her party didn't. One entry states: "George lost his child"; the next, simply, "laid by and buried it." Sara Perkins—or Grandma Perkins, as she was better known—settled in Tillamook and lived until 1912, having reached the ripe old age of 92 years, 8 months, and 3 days. Her framed portrait hangs behind the reception desk at the Tillamook County Pioneer Museum, just one of the dozens of stern images of early settlers that line the museum's walls and stairways, each with its own story.

The museum fills all three floors of the old courthouse. Next to the well-stocked pioneer workshop, visitors can peer into Joseph Champion's curious "stump house." Champion was Tillamook's first white settler, and when he got here in 1851 he set up housekeeping in the stump of a big hollow spruce tree he called his "castle." The stump here is a replica, but you can get an idea of just how big Champion's castle really was by looking closely at the picture of the real stump; it shows three women standing in the "doorway" holding their outstretched arms tip-to-tip across the opening.

Much of Alex Walker's natural history collection fills the large old courtroom on the museum's second floor. Walker was the museum's first curator, and he had a personal specimen collection of more than 3,200 birds and 1,100 mammals. What didn't fit here he donated to the Museum of Natural History at Oregon State University in Corvallis. But it's hard to imagine that it's not all here.

Don't go to the basement alone—a two-headed dinosaur lurks there.

Swans, beavers, wolves, bears, penguins, and even a moose and a bald eagle are given plenty of room, and many animals are "posed" in dioramas that show their relationship, as predator or dinner, to others in the animal kingdom.

Novelties exist among the serious natural history presentations. Atop an antique curio cabinet, for instance, there's a box of 46 species of bird eggs, point-side down, hanging at varying heights from fishing line. Nearby, a display titled "Colors in Nature" demonstrates how red, blue, yellow, green, and the combination of black and white appear in nature. The "yellow" box contains a Tillamook canary, a yellow Florida sulphur butterfly, a yellow Cuban tropical tree snail, and, from Nevada, a piece of yellow sulphur ore. In the exhibit case titled "The Rare, Odd, and Beautiful in Nature," look for the hummingbird nest that was built on a clothesline on someone's back porch, using clothespins for its structure.

The museum basement, however, holds the most charming, if dustiest, local treasures. At the bottom of the stairs there's a 1909 Buick, a crank model with a wooden "dash" and headlights that look curiously like portholes. Also, someone saved the stagecoach that was used on the North Yamhill and Tillamook Stage Line. It ran from 1906 through 1911 and was advertised as the "cheapest, shortest, quickest, and best" way to travel, but we noticed that no claims were made about how comfortable the trip would be.

Meandering through the rest of the basement rooms, you'll confront a talking Smokey Bear, Grandma's life-size kitchen with lumberjack Dad sitting down to a breakfast of bacon and eggs, a roomful of washtubs, and a display of ocean finds, including a large seagrass ball created on the ocean floor and a piece of driftwood that looks exactly like a two-headed baby dinosaur.

Tillamook County Pioneer Museum • 2106 Second Street, Tillamook, Oregon 97141 • (503) 842-4553
Admission: $1. Hours: Mar 15–Sept 30: Mon–Sat 8am–5pm, Sun 12pm–5pm; Oct 1–Mar 15: closed Mon. To get there: The museum is at the junction of US 101 and State Highway 6. It's a large building with a logging donkey out front.

Name That Tree

WILSONVILLE
Grove of the States

ere's a chance to take a break from freeway driving at a rest stop that features something other than the usual picnic tables, restrooms, free coffee, and designated dog-walking areas. Start at the wooden sign that lists the 50 states and stretch your legs on the short, circular path that meanders through a grove of trees in which you'll find a sample of each state's official tree. Then get back in the car and quiz your travelmates on the tree names and on how in Johnny Appleseed's name they get them all to grow here.

Few of us know all the state capitals, let alone the state trees, so there's an educational opportunity here. A palm tree represents South Carolina, and an Eastern white pine comes from Maine. Couldn't Virginia, New York, and Wisconsin have been more imaginative? They all chose the same tree: the sugar maple. Same with Guam, Hawaii, Puerto Rico, and the Virgin Islands; they're all represented by pagoda trees. Washington's Western hemlock is here, along with Oregon's Douglas fir.

And you thought palm trees could grow only in Florida.

Grove of the States

Admission: Free. **Hours:** Open 24 hours. **To get there:** The grove is at the rest stop at Mile 282 on I-5 South. It's just past Wilsonville, if you're traveling south from Portland.

Appendix

More Museums, Collections, and Roadside Curiosities

Agriculture

Central Washington Agricultural Museum, 4508 Main Street, Union Gap, Washington 98903 • (509) 457-8735
A large farm equipment collection in an outdoor setting.

Animals

North American Wildlife Exhibit, PO Box 644, Winthrop, Washington 98862 • (509) 996-2330
The price of admission is pretty stiff, but if you want to get really close to a lot of stuffed wild animals and animal skulls, go on in.

Art

Bellevue Art Museum, 301 Bellevue Square, Bellevue, Washington 98004 (206) 454-3322
Changing exhibits include a recent George Tsutakawa retrospective. Located on the third floor of a bustling mall.

Frye Art Museum, 704 Terry Avenue, Seattle, Washington 98114 (206) 622-9250
Nineteenth-century European paintings and three generations of Wyeths. Admission is always free.

Portland Art Museum, 1219 SW Park Avenue, Portland, Oregon 97205 (503) 226-2811
Permanent collections at this contemporary downtown landmark range from the tribal art of Cameroon to prehistoric Chinese artifacts.

Seattle-Tacoma International Airport, PO Box 68727, Seattle, Washington 98168 • (206) 433-4629
Scattered throughout the main terminal are pieces by such well-known artists as Robert Rauschenberg, Frank Stella, and Louise Nevelson. A gallery near the chapel features glass pieces by artists from the Pilchuck glass school.

Shakespeare Art Museum, 460 B Street, Ashland, Oregon 97520
(503) 325-6311
Artist Hannah Tompkins has made it her life's work to create surreal,
impressionistic visions of the Bard's plays.

Aviation

Evergreen AirVenture Museum, 3850 Three Mile Lane, McMinnville
Airport, McMinnville, Oregon 97128 • (503)472-9361
Wealthy entrepreneur Delford Smith is assembling a huge collection of
historic airplanes. Among them is the *Spruce Goose*, the famous 140-ton
wooden "flying boat" built by Howard Hughes.

Oregon Aviation and Space Museum
90377 Boeing Drive, Eugene Airport, Eugene, Oregon 97402
(503) 461-1101

Children

Portland Children's Museum, 3037 SW 2nd Avenue, Portland, Oregon
97201 • (503) 823-2227
Pint-size accessories and interactive exhibits emphasize fun and learning.

Seattle Children's Museum, Seattle Center, Seattle, Washington 98109
(206) 441-1767
Hands-on exhibits and learning center for children of all ages.

Historical

Most every town, city, and county has its own historical museum. There are
far too many for us to list here, but we urge you to seek them out. You'll not
only learn about a community's past, but you may just stumble upon a surprising, unpublicized treasure. And if you do, let us know!

Nordic Heritage Museum, 3014 NW 67th Street, Seattle, Washington
98117 • (206) 789-5707
Exhibits include photographs, maritime equipment, costumes, and other
memorabilia of Nordic settlers in the United States. A 9-foot-tall taxidermied
Alaskan brown bear stands guard.

Oregon Historical Society, 1230 SW Park Avenue, Portland, Oregon
97205 • (503) 222-1741
Among the holdings in the museum archives: one of the three largest collections of presidential campaign material—some 8,000 buttons, banners,
ribbons, placards, and other memorabilia dating back to George Washington.

Logging

**Camp Seven Logger's Museum, Concrete, Washington 98237
(206) 853-8304**

Herb Larsen's new little museum highlights the logging culture and equipment he grew up with. Items include Billy Mason's folding engineer's table, branding irons used to identify timber, and a "filing shack" where each large saw was assigned to an individual logger. In an alley off Concrete's main street.

Camp 6 Logging Museum, N 54th and Pearl Street, Tacoma, Washington 98401 • (206) 752-0047

Reconstructed logging camp, logging machinery, railroad cars and a steam engine.

**Collier Logging Museum, Collier State Park, Chiloquin, Oregon 97624
(503) 783-2471**

Claims to have the United States's largest logging equipment collection.

**Forks Timber Museum, PO Box 973, Forks, Washington 98331
(206) 374-9663**

This museum, built by the local high school's carpentry class, has exhibits on logging, homesteaders, and coastal Indians. On Highway 101 across from the Forks airport.

Maritime

Bremerton Naval Museum, 130 Washington Avenue, Bremerton, Washington 98310 • (206) 479-7447

Odyssey, Pier 66, Seattle, Washington 98101

A new maritime museum in the works for Pier 66 at the north end of Seattle's waterfront. Scheduled to open sometime in 1995 or 1996.

Oregon Maritime Center and Museum, 113 SW Front Avenue, Portland, Oregon 97204 • (503) 224-7724

Mining

Baker County Visitor Center and Chamber of Commerce, 490 Campbell Street, Baker City, Oregon 97814 • (503) 523-3356

Baker City was once known as Queen City of the Mines and boasts more than 135 buildlings on the National Historic Register. The second floor of the visitor center displays early mining and agricultural artifacts, pioneer household goods, and historic photographs.

U.S. National Bank, Main Street, Baker City, Oregon 97814
(503) 523-7791
The lobby of the Baker City branch of U.S. Bank National houses Oregon's largest display of gold. Included among the samples is the famed 80.4-ounce "Armstrong Nugget."

Native American

Many city, and county museums include the history of the Native American tribes that originally lived in the region. There are also tribal-run museums.

Makah Cultural and Research Center, PO Box 95, Neah Bay, Washington 98357 • (206) 645-2711
Houses more than 55,000 artifacts from a Makah village, buried 500 years ago by a mudslide and discovered in 1970. The Ozette village became one of the most important digs in North America. Full-scale replicas of canoes and a longhouse.

Museum at Warm Springs, PO Box C, Warm Springs, Oregon 97761
(503) 553-3331
Explores the culture and history of the Wasco, Paiute, and Warm Springs people, who make up the confederated Tribes of the Warm Springs Indian Reservation.

Suquamish Museum, 15838 Sandy Hook Road, Suquamish, Washington 98392 • (206) 598-3311
Devoted to displaying and studying Salish culture. Nearby, at St. Peter's Catholic Mission Church, is the grave of Chief Sealth.

Roadside Curiosities

Bair Drug and Hardware Co. Living Museum, 1617 Lafayette Street, Steilacoom, Washington 98388 • (206) 588-9668
Bair Drug was once a soda fountain, drugstore, and hardware store on the trolley line. A restaurant, complete with old-fashioned soda fountain, still operates here, and display cases along the wall are stocked with turn-of-the-century pharmacy items.

Bear Hut Family Restaurant, 623 9th Street, Benton City, Washington 99320 • (509) 588-3142
There's a barber chair in the men's room and, leaning on one wall, a 1929 motorcycle that belonged to a Whidbey Island postman who used it on his route. Shelves hold a cream separator, an old checkerboard, an airplane propeller, a bottle of Rawleigh's Anti-Pain Oil, and more.

Eaglemount Rockeries, south of Port Townsend on Discovery Bay, near the junction of Old Route 104 and Route 113

The draw is a series of miniature scenes made of rocks and plastic accessories. What these scenes—including a lighthouse, castle, Old West town, pyramids, Noah's Ark, and windmill—lack in technical finesse is more than made up for by their enthusiastic charm.

Science

Pacific Science Center, Seattle Center, Seattle, Washington 98109 (206) 443-2880

The Pacific Science Center has many fine, instructive exhibits. You can ride a bicycle on a thin circular rail high above the heads of people below. You are kept from certain doom only by the force of gravity acting on a huge counterweight attached to the bike. It's perfectly safe, of course, but it always gives something of a jolt nonetheless.

WISTEC (Willamette Science and Technology Center), 2300 Centennial Boulevard, Eugene, Oregon 97401 • (503) 484-9027

Hands-on science and technology exhibits and planetarium.

Wild West

Clymer Museum, 416 N Pearl, Ellensburg, Washington 98926 (509) 962-6416

Dedicated entirely to the distinguished Western art painter John Clymer.

Pendleton Underground Tour, 37 SW Emigrant Avenue, Pendleton, Oregon 97801 • (503) 276-0730

Visitors can take guided tours through some of the re-created and refurbished underground areas and see what Pendleton may have looked like in its bawdy, wild days.

General Tourism Numbers

Oregon Tourism Division (800) 547-7842; in Oregon (800) 233-3306

Washington State Tourism Development Division (206) 586-2102 or (206) 586-2088

Credits

Washington

4: Courtesy of Bob Weatherly.

7: Photograph by Sandra Hoover.

9, 10: Drawings by Constance Perenyi.

16: Courtesy of the Vintage Telephone Equipment Museum.

18: Courtesy of the Moore House.

20: Reprinted with permission from Rocky Mountain House Books.

25: Courtesy of the Boeing Company.

27: Drawing by Kelly Balcomb-Bartok.

31: Courtesy of the Maryhill Museum.

33: Courtesy of the Colville Tribal Museum.

35: Courtesy of the Bureau of Reclamation, United States Department of the Interior.

38: Reprinted with permission of Washington State Historical Society.

39: Photograph by Karna Steelquist.

42: Courtesy of the World Kite Museum.

46: Photograph by Karna Steelquist.

49: Courtesy of Monte Holm.

50: Courtesy of the Snoqualmie Valley Historical Society.

52: Reprinted with permission of Washington State Capitol Museum.

56: Reprinted with permission of the Jefferson County Historical Society.

59, 60: Courtesy of the Puget Sound Coast Artillery Museum.

65, 69: Photograph by Karna Steelquist.

71: Photograph by Lisa Stone. Reprinted courtesy of *Seattle Weekly*.

76: Photograph by Karna Steelquist.

84: Courtesy of the Coast Guard Museum.

86: Courtesy of *Seattle Weekly*.

88: Courtesy of the Kingdome Sports Museum.

90: Photograph by Hegg, neg. # Hegg100. Reprinted with permission from Special Collections Division, University of Washington Libraries.

92: Drawing courtesy of the Last Resort Fire Department.

93: Courtesy of the Museum of Flight

98: Photograph by Karna Steelquist.

101: Courtesy of the Phoebe Hearst Museum of Anthropology, University of California at Berkeley.

103: Courtesy of Seattle Art Museum.

106, 107: Drawing courtesy of the Balch Collection, Seattle Public Library.

108: Drawing courtesy of the Puget Sound Antique Radio Association.

111: Photograph by Karna Steelquist.

112: Courtesy of the Henry Art Gallery, University of Washington.

117: Courtesy of Vintage Telephone Equipment Museum.

119, 120: Photograph by Karna Steelquist.

123: Courtesy of the Wing Luke Asian Museum.

125: Photograph by Karna Steelquist.

127: Courtesy of the Cheney Cowles Museum.

132: Courtesy of the Steilacoom Tribal Cultural Center.

133: Courtesy of the Skamania County Historical Society and Museum.

136: Courtesy of Tacoma Art Museum.

138: Courtesy of Washington State Historical Society.

143: Photograph by Karna Steelquist.

146: Courtesy of North Central Washington Museum.

153: Photograph from the Warren G. Magnuson Collection, neg. # 3181-4. Reprinted with permission from Manuscripts and University Archives Division, University of Washington Libraries.

Oregon

157: Courtesy of the Oregon Shakespeare Festival.

159: Drawing courtesy of Columbia River Maritime Museum.

162: Courtesy of Clatsop County Historical Society.

164: Courtesy of Aurora Colony Museum.

166: Courtesy of the Bureau of Land Management.

172: Courtesy of the High Desert Museum.

176: Courtesy of Cottage Grove Museum.

179: Courtesy of Fly Fishing Museum.

180: Courtesy of Jerry's Rogue River Museum.

181: Courtesty of Harriet Baskas.

184: Courtesy of Hood River County Historical Museum.

186: Photograph by Peter Britt, neg. # 10049, courtesy of the Southern Oregon Historical Society.

188: Courtesy of Kam Wah Chung & Co. Museum.

189: Courtesy of the Favell Museum of Western Art and Indian Artifacts.

194: Courtesy of the Southern Oregon Historical Society.

195: Courtesy of Dr. Paul Jensen.

199: Reprinted with permission of the Howdyshell Collection.

201: Courtesy of the Umatilla County Historical Society.

203: Courtesy of the American Advertising Museum.

205: Courtesy of Cowboys Then & Now Museum.

208: Photograph by Pete Liddell, courtesy of Metro Washington Park Zoo.

212: Photograph by Karna Steelquist.

214: Courtesy of Oregon Museum of Science and Industry.

216: Neg. # 4853-2. Reprinted with permission of the Oregon Historical Society.

218: Courtesy of Stark's Vacuum Cleaners.

220: Courtesy of Van Calvin's Manikin Restoration.

223: Courtesy of World Forestry Center.

227: Courtesy of Mary Catherine Lamb.

230: Drawing courtesy of Gilbert House Children's Museum.

232: Courtesy of the Prewitt-Allen Museum of Middle Eastern Archaeology, Western Baptist College.

233: Courtesy of Seaside Museum & Historical Society.

235: Courtesy of White's Electronics.

238, 239: Courtesy of Tillamook County Pioneer Museum.

Index